Corporate Communications Networks

J E Lane

PUBLISHED BY NCC PUBLICATIONS

British Library Cataloguing in Publication Data

Lane, J. E.
 Corporate communications networks.
 1. Telecommunication
 I. Title
 384   HE7631

ISBN 0-85012-413-1

©THE NATIONAL COMPUTING CENTRE LIMITED, 1984

All rights reserved. No part of this publication may be reproduced, stored in a retrieval system, or transmitted, in any form or by any means, without the prior permission of The National Computing Centre.

First published in 1984 by:
NCC Publications, The National Computing Centre Limited, Oxford Road, Manchester M1 7ED, England.

Typeset in 11pt Times Roman by UPS Blackburn Limited, 76-80 Northgate, Blackburn, Lancashire, and printed by Hobbs the Printers of Southampton.

ISBN 0-85012-413-1

Preface

Many of the larger organisations in the UK, with several operating sites, have long-term strategies for carrying all their inter-site traffic (voice, data, text, and, in some cases, facsimile and video) on private 'wide-area' corporate communications networks. This represents a major change from the time when speech and data networks developed along separate routes, and, as such, requires a complete review of the organisation's communications requirements.

The growing availability of digital services over the next five to ten years is likely to encourage many other organisations to start thinking in terms of wide-area integrated networking. This thinking will be considerably helped by knowing how other organisations have approached the problem.

This book addresses the issue by first reviewing the current state of corporate communications in the UK and then examining the strategic opportunities of today and tomorrow for the planning of corporate networks.

By its very definition 'corporate' communications implies *the bringing together of the communications needs of the organisation and expressing them collectively as a single requirement.* No single book could hope to be exhaustive in this task, nor indeed would it be possible to attempt to define the individual communications requirements of the multiplicity of business interests which exist today. However, there are in the world of business telecommunications, as in many other innovative fields at any one time, common conceptual threads which can be woven into a distinguishable pattern.

This book attempts to establish the likely shape of corporate communications in the UK over the next few years and from this to derive a coherent set of common guidelines for strategic planners.

In presenting this information it is recognised that corporate telecommunications today embraces a very broad spectrum of technology and applications. The limitations of a book of this nature have meant that in many instances it has only been possible to take a superficial look at the current techniques and offerings. The reader is referred to the Bibliography as a source of further information and background material.

John Lane

Acknowledgements

I would like to thank all the individuals and organisations who assisted in the preparation of this book. In particular I am indebted to the following for reviewing the initial draft and for their varied and helpful comments:

Ashwin Vara	CEGB
Brian West	NCC
Don Mildenhall	BT
Geoff Johnson	Barclays Bank
Peter Cordukes	ICI
Ron Pontefract	Rowntree Mackintosh
Stuart McLean	Barclays Bank

The collaboration of the following organisations is also recorded with grateful thanks:

Allied Breweries Beer Division
Allied Breweries Group Telecomms
Barclays Bank
Blue Circle Industries
British Steel
British Telecom: National Networks
CEGB
Co-op Bank
Ferranti
ICI Corporate Management Services
Lucas Group
Peugeot-Talbot
Rowntree Mackintosh

Sainsbury's
Trusthouse Forte
Turner Newall

The Centre acknowledges with thanks the support provided by the Electronics and Avionics Requirements Board (EARB) for the project from which this publication derives.

Contents

	Page
Preface	
Acknowledgements	
1 **Introduction**	13
2 **Where Are We Now?**	21
The Picture	21
The Cost Question	22
Remedies of the Past	24
3 **The Need to Communicate**	25
Introduction	25
Types of Communication	25
Voice	25
Data Communications	25
Text Communications	26
Facsimile	26
Viewdata	27
Video	28
Process Control	28
Personal Computing	29
Impact on Communications Services	29
4 **The Next Five Years**	31
Introduction	31

Carrier Services	31
Packet SwitchStream (PSS)	33
Integrated Digital Access (IDA)	35
X-Stream Services	35
MegaStream	37
KiloStream	40
SatStream	43
Mercury Communications	43
Telex/Teletex	45
Conferencing	48

5 Options for the Future   51

Introduction	51
Integrated Services Digital Network (ISDN)	51
ISDN User Interfaces	53
Voice/Data Integration Opportunities	54
Voice and Data Requirements	56
Transmission Technologies – Trends	57
Network Switching Technologies – Trends	57
Interfacing and Signalling – Trends	58
Current Developments (Voice/Data)	59
National Digital Private Circuit Network	59
ISDN in the UK	61
IDA Pilot Service	61
IDA Signalling	64
Satellite Business Networks	67
Business Communications Systems	67

6 Integrated Voice and Data in the Office   69

An Overview	69
Integration of Services	70
PABX Developments	74
Integrated Network Services	75
Integration of Services in Private Networks	76

7 Network Strategy for the Eighties   81

Introduction	81
Why a Strategy?	81

	The Benefits of a Strategy	82
	Organisational Issues	83
	Organising for Information Technology (IT)	84
	Developing a Corporate IT Strategy	85
	Resolve Strategic Issues First	85
	Design the Operational Management Group	88
8	**Elements of a Communications Strategy**	91
	Introduction	91
	Defining the Goal	91
	Standards in IT	93
	Intercept Strategy	94
	The Integration Question	95
	Data Services	95
	Voice/Data Services	96
	Text Services	96
	Image Services	96
	Evolution of Integrated Services	96
	The ISDN Connection	99
	Private ISDN Networks	100
	Local Area Networks	100
	Planning to Meet the Goal	101
9	**A Strategic Plan**	105
	Introduction	105
	The Organisation	105
	The Objectives	106
	The Overall Strategy	106
	Migrate to Open Systems Interconnection	106
	Consolidate all Separate Data Networks	109
	Open up the Data Network	110
	Exploit the New Opportunities	111
	Sub-Strategies	114
	Voice Services	114
	Data Services	120
	A Degree of Integration	121
	The Strategy in Brief	123
	Overall Strategy	123
	Sub-Strategies	123

Which First? 124
Private or Public ISDN Networks? 126

Bibliography 129

1 Introduction

Organisations never seem to outgrow their need for increased quantities of information. As the typical business organisation expands its horizons and capabilities, and in doing so becomes more complex, executives at all levels realise that they must have access to more and more information relating to all aspects of their operation. This quest for expanding information has inevitably led to the increased collection and storage of information in virtually all departments within many organisations.

As these corporate information bases proliferate, more data must be accessed, analysed, and presented to top management in an understandable and usable form. Because most business information is today handled by automated systems, the ability to deliver data where and when needed becomes an essential and crucial requirement.

The delivery of automated information within an organisation basically requires a reliable transport mechanism which is widely available to all users. This type of transport mechanism is commonly known as the corporate communications network since it provides the vital link which facilitates the flow of information throughout the organisation and allows management to gather the information required to run the business.

Such a network (Figure 1.1) may be required to support a wide range of devices (eg mainframes, terminals, distributed processors, local area networks and PABXs) and provide a variety of communications services (eg data communications, voice communications, message switching, electronic mail, telex/Teletex, viewdata,

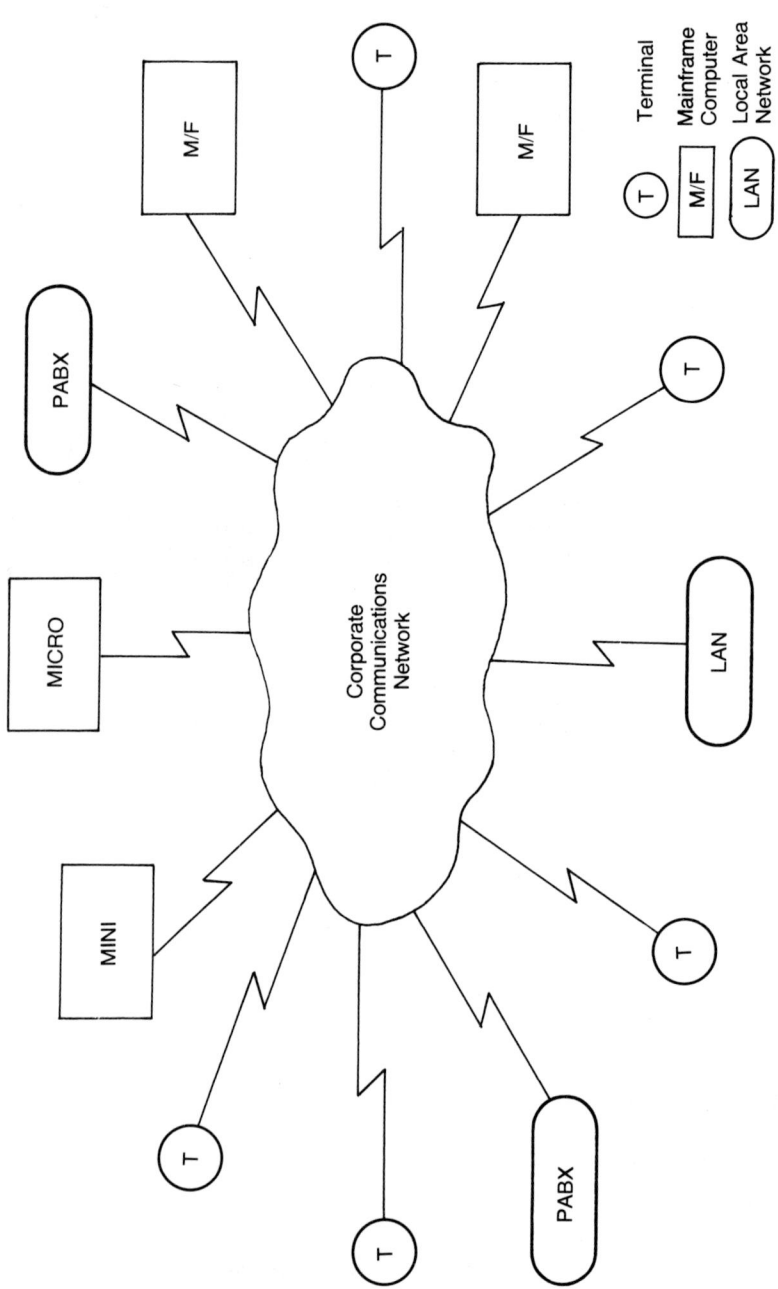

Figure 1.1 Corporate Communications Network

INTRODUCTION

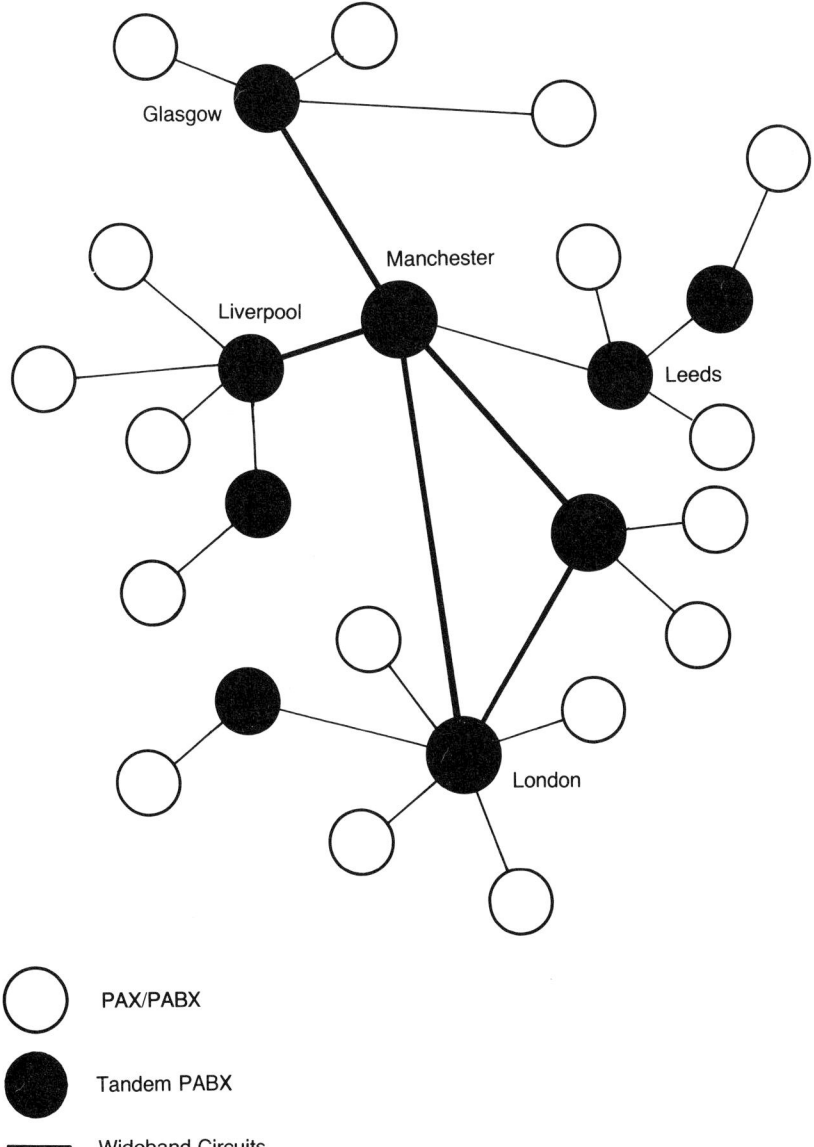

○ PAX/PABX

● Tandem PABX

▬ Wideband Circuits

Figure 1.2   Voice Network

facsimile and personal computing). Where day-to-day communication traffic volumes have been identified as significant, corporate voice and data networks have traditionally been established as the most cost-effective solution.

A typical voice network is shown in Figure 1.2. Such a network:

— comprises a number of mixed PAXs and PABXs at various locations throughout the country (30 to 50 typical) linked by private point-to-point circuits via tandem switches located at the main centres;

— provides direct dialling facilities to (say, up to 10,000) extensions and handles many thousands of calls per day with a high proportion of these across the network;

— in addition to voice services, is likely to provide private telex/teleprinter services.

Present or future developments may also include the extension or introduction of facsimile transmission, message switching and voice store-and-forward facilities.

Cost-effectiveness of the voice network can be improved by extensive traffic monitoring, by using the latest technologies and techniques, such as electronic exchanges, and by educating users in the effective use of the network.

The use of call information logging can lead to the optimisation of exchange and switchboard facilities, encourage responsible telephone usage, and above all provide a basis for effective network planning. Information on the spread of traffic loads over specific routes may well identify a need for out-of-area wideband links as a basis for further cost savings; in this respect many organisations have implemented wideband circuits (12 channel groups) and supergroups to minimise the number of connections over common routes.

A typical data network is shown in Figure 1.3. Such a network:

— comprises distributed minis, remote terminals and host mainframe linked by private circuit point-to-point and multipoint (Tariff T and S3 circuits) connections with speeds ranging from 2.4 to 9.6 Kbit/s.

INTRODUCTION

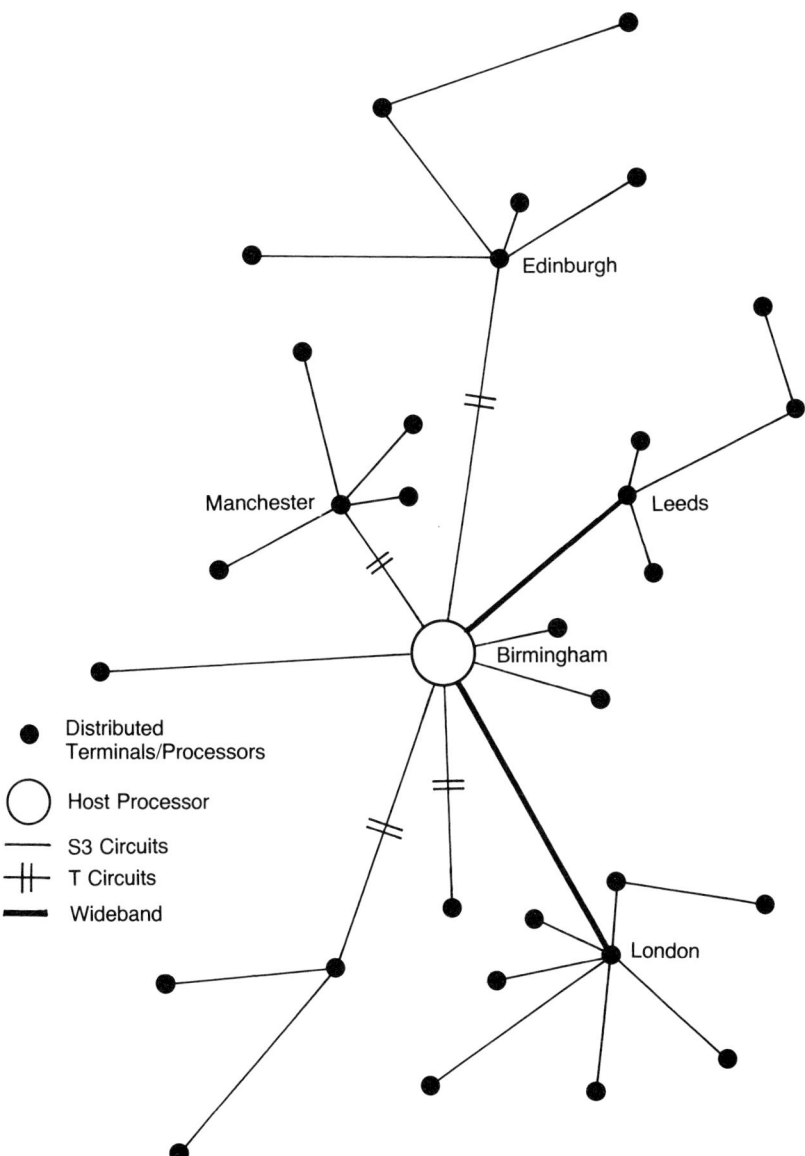

Figure 1.3 Data Network

In addition to private circuit connections, PSTN access may be provided for dial-up data communications and PSTN standby facilities in the event of private circuit failure. Where circuit loadings are sufficient, wideband circuits may be used between main centres.

Such a network primarily supports data processing facilities (ie on-line, batch and RJE processing) but in many cases may also support message switching and viewdata services. Present and future developments are likely to include the growth of interactive systems, further decentralisation, and development of distributed office and database systems.

The cost-effectiveness of the data network can be maintained by the adoption of new technologies such as statistical multiplexers, by reviewing the network topology to suit changing needs and by the establishment and maintenance of performance and cost criteria through effective network management.

Although separate voice and data networks have been depicted, it makes sense from a corporate point of view to combine whatever facilities are appropriate to achieve direct cost benefits. It is often common practice to use voice and data channels in parallel on wideband links between main centres; speech circuits for data transmission outside normal office hours; and backward channels for message switching, etc.

Some of the main objectives for developing corporate networks along these lines may include:

— to save money by the economies of scale of large networks;
— to respond quickly to organisational changes;
— to provide flexibility for future expansion in the number of network users and in the utilisation of different network services;
— to facilitate centralised network control;
— to allow new users to gain rapid and low-cost access to the network;
— to support new services and new technologies.

INTRODUCTION

But in practice are these objectives being realised? In particular, are the potential cost savings of such networks achieved? What is the anticipated impact of the new and emerging services on the corporate communications facilities to be provided? These are the two fundamental questions addressed in Chapter 2 and Chapter 3. Chapter 2 briefly examines where we are now, and Chapter 3 provides a summary of requirements for future communications within organisations.

For more than a quarter of a century, telecommunications has grown rapidly. Advances in technology have served not only to meet, but also to stimulate that growth; for example, with the development of submarine cable technology in the 1950s and the use of commercial satellites from the mid-1960s.

Until the mid-1970s, user requirements for data transmission were largely met by facilities available on the switched telephone and telex networks, and on analogue leased circuits. For multi-destination traffic there was the analogue switched telephone service which could also handle data traffic to many worldwide destinations and for text transfer there was telex. The larger corporate organisations operating in the multinational environment could, on routes where traffic volumes were large enough, opt for private leased circuits and use them for voice, text, data and facsimile.

We are now in a period where choice is the keyword and telecommunications service suppliers are actively working to meet, and moreover anticipate, the often highly specialised needs of the modern business community.

Today the number and variety of telecommunications hardware and service options available is accelerating rapidly due to:

— the continuing decline in the cost of the silicon chip, and its increasing reliability and robustness;

— the explosive growth in both public and private network services;

— the convergence of telecommunications, computer and office equipment technologies.

Chapter 4 reviews the recent developments in public and private network services and examines the subsequent trend in development over the next five years. In Chapter 5 the options for the convergence of the information technologies are discussed. In Chapter 6 the integration of voice and data services in the office, where the convergence technology is expected to have greatest impact, is considered in greater depth.

Many of the new opportunities offered by today's telecommunications hardware and service facilities stem from increasing the level of integration between activities within organisations and by the imaginative adoption of new services to enable existing activities to be performed more effectively. To realise the opportunities in these two ways, it is necessary to develop a strategy which builds the foundations for corporate integration to take place, and at the same time, take a pragmatic view of the new facilities as they become available.

Chapter 7 examines such an approach by first considering the benefits of having a strategy, the organisational and strategic issues involved and the basic requirements of operational management. In Chapter 8 the elements of a strategy are defined and discussed in detail.

The final chapter of the book, Chapter 9, presents a 'strategic plan' which pulls together the many facets of the communications issue discussed in the earlier chapters. These, combined with the experiences of many organisations, provide guidelines for the future planning of corporate communications networks. This is the basis of the strategy – its success can only depend upon organisations having both the imagination and resolution to seize the opportunities.

2 Where Are We Now?

THE PICTURE

The rapid development of new telecommunications technology, although of benefit to most organisations, has sometimes created several problems. These are often not directly related to the deficiencies of the systems but are the result of the potential benefits not being fully realised. For example, facility utilisation checks on Stored Program Control (SPC) switchboards have shown that typically no more than 15% of the many facilities available are in fact utilised, and despite the availability of Call Information Logging facilities on many SPC PABXs, many managers either ignore them or cannot understand them and continue to pay higher than necessary charges for telephone calls.

In other areas a considerable amount of management time is wasted in travelling to and from meetings; little attention is being given to the opportunities of modern teleconferencing facilities which can offer an acceptable alternative. But, above all, the potential of the public carrier services, eg wideband and digital services, has not been fully realised in the planning of corporate communications networks.

Consequently, as shown by the telecommunications services currently used by many UK organisations, it appears that many services are in fact provided far in excess of actual traffic load requirements of the organisation. Such a situation gives rise to high and unnecessary costs and inhibits the modification of existing services to allow the development of new applications and future services.

Development of corporate telecommunications services along these lines has resulted in the provision of separate voice and data networks and in many instances even separate text networks.

Often such networks will overlap considerably in the provision of services from a central site to the many common locations within the corporate geography. This in effect means that for these situations the provision of all public and/or private carrier services has been duplicated, resulting in substantial cost increase but without the benefit of increased traffic volumes.

If it had been planned that both types of traffic be carried on the same network then more efficient services would have resulted. Other benefits would follow, including savings due to 'bulk buying', centralised management of network, etc.

The picture that emerges is one of a proliferation of communications services in this form. This has been necessitated to a large extent by the lack of effective control of communications as a corporate resource. Data networks have evolved to satisfy immediate needs with little or no consideration of overall system architecture. This may be attributed to a pressing requirement to implement the service quickly, the lack of corporate management policy, the lack of standards, and an attempt to obtain the right equipment at the right price at the right time. Speech networks have traditionally been established to fulfil basic requirements but, as organisation growth has occurred, the networks have not developed to match fresh business needs.

Although these problems can predominantly be traced to the user organisation, in fairness it must be recognised that one major problem has been the lack of effective management control facilities on both data and voice systems on the market. Without such facilities, data and telecommunications management has, for example, been unable to fully analyse the traffic carried by the network at any particular period of the day to initiate more efficient and cost-effective use of services.

THE COST QUESTION

A potential for achieving cost savings in both services and equipment can therefore be identified by adopting a corporate approach, but how can these savings be made? It is first necessary to establish the present cost of telecommunications to the organisation. It is essential to pose the question 'Do we know how much we are currently paying for our existing services?'

An answer to this question is often lacking due to an absence of central co-ordination of paperwork, organisational fragmentation, and above all lack of management need. Many organisations have been surprised at the size of the telephone bill alone: £30M to £45M per annum is typical for central government and large banking institutions, whereas £2M to £3M per annum is likely in manufacturing organisations with a turnover of around £1000M. To remedy this situation, by carrying out an investigation of the overall organisational situation, often requires considerable effort and time. One example – that of a large manufacturing company with 1000 sites in the UK – involved the expenditure of 45 man-weeks to arrive at the correct figure.

Apart from the cost question, visits to a cross-section of industry and commerce reveal that for many organisations there is a lack of detailed appreciation of the systems in use, little knowledge of the degree of proliferation of services throughout the organisation and, more often than not, inadequate awareness of the actual use made of the services available to the organisation. Furthermore there is often no knowledge of the spare capacity available on the systems or of the need to extend systems as appropriate to ensure the continuity of services for the future. The following observations may be made:

— more than 80% of PABX replacements are necessitated by crisis rather than by logical planning or development;

— recent experience has shown that a high proportion of BT invoices are incorrect, resulting in either over- or undercharging for many organisations, more often the former;

— incorrect design parameters for company networks often result in the inability of the company to grow and provide the additional services within the necessary timescales;

— for many companies the development of integrated office services has been frustrated because of the inability of existing systems to cope with the additional load.

REMEDIES OF THE PAST

Over the past three to four years, many organisations have attempted to remedy the situation described above by taking on improvements in technology. These have included the use of new stored program control PABXs, telex message switching systems, communicating word processing equipment, advanced facsimile equipment, and conferencing facilities.

Unfortunately, for many organisations the real benefits of such new services have not been fully realised. There may have been a lack of successful training and user awareness. More importantly, an incorrect system may have been chosen through lack of technical appreciation, through market pressures, or through lack of a logical and planned approach and an overall strategy which addresses the particular business needs of the organisation. This important area becomes the predominant theme of the final chapters.

3 The Need to Communicate

INTRODUCTION

In this chapter, the requirements for communications within organisations are briefly examined to indicate the scope planning has to cover. In the next chapter, the options for new ways of communicating are explored. It is useful to survey the types of communication which may need to be handled.

TYPES OF COMMUNICATION

Voice

Telephone communications is likely to remain, at least for the foreseeable future, the most commonly encountered vehicle for communicating in the office. It will thus remain very significant in any communications planning. New developments (such as cellular radio) are likely to lead to a significant increase in future use of voice since it is usually desirable to link radio systems to traditional voice telephone systems.

Data Communications

Most organisations have diverse data terminal networks covering a variety of data processing applications. It is likely that the conventional DP terminal-based system will continue to be the predominant form of office automation for many years. This form of communication is therefore fundamental to corporate business requirements. Hand-held micros (data capture) via public network links could be a significant area of increased utilisation in the future.

Text Communications

This category embraces the growing form of communications between word processors and intelligent printers as well as the more traditional telex 'messaging' service and the developing Teletex service. Communicating word processors and intelligent printers are often treated as a form of data communications, whereas separate electronic message systems cater for transmission of telex and Teletex messages.

Teletex is a worldwide standard for electronic messaging which will soon be offered as a standard feature on many word processors. It offers a much more rapid standard communication of text messages than does telex.

Telex has existed for a number of years and because of its widely installed base can be regarded as a mature service which will exist for many years. The introduction of improved terminals and network services will provide new facilities and advantages for the user. However, little growth in network size is expected during the remainder of the 1980s and a gradual decline is anticipated in the 1990s as Teletex takes over its role with the growth of electronic mail systems based on inter-word processor communication.

The continuing role of telex services together with the likely effects of Teletex developments clearly need to be taken into account in communications planning.

Facsimile

The most usual form of use for fax message transmission today is dial-up over the PSTN to provide for the transmission of document contents between sites in the UK and overseas. Fax message transmission has not so far gained popular support; this is largely because of the machines and standards traditionally used to transmit fax messages. Essentially the analogue transmission was slow and the quality of reproduction was poor. The advent of digital fax within the last ten years has led to a significant improvement in these areas and has encouraged the acceptance of fax.

The other significant factor is the adoption of standards for compatibility. Any fax machine which conforms to the established standard (Groups 1, 2 and 3) can communicate with any other in the same category. Digital interfaces derived from basic Group 3 digital fax open up the possibilities for further developments. Interfacing with data networks is now a possibility which will add a capability to an existing communications system by extending the range of terminals and messages to include typewritten and handwritten materials, diagrams, etc. Bit rates of up to 14.4 Kbit/s are standard with options up to 19.2 Kbit/s.

Another significant activity which will contribute to fax development will be the formulation and ratification of the Group 4 compatibility standard by CCITT during 1984 to cater for fax at speeds higher than those currently available under Group 3. Also under consideration are machines which will facilitate mixed-mode operation; for example, Teletex and fax, text and graphics and store-and-forward capacity will allow the development of such functions as mailbox and interworking between telex, Teletex and fax.

So the future for fax looks healthy, particularly with the increase in transmission speeds together with improvements in the production of printed output document.

Viewdata

Videotex (or Viewdata) has taken a long time to win widespread approval but at last there are signs in the UK that videotex is emerging from the doldrums. The concept of taking a TV set, adding an electronic keyboard and connecting them via a telephone link to a central computer holding an information database is well established. But it has taken more than ten years for videotex to come of age.

The original belief that Prestel would appeal primarily to the domestic market fell flat on its face. Fortunately, BT foresaw a business demand and made provision for Closed User Groups, in effect the first private as opposed to public videotex systems. This approach boosted business user interest in videotex by providing impetus for the development of two-way communications, communications with existing databases, and running applications held on the mainframe computer. This brought the benefits of computing to a much wider audience through the availability of comparatively low-cost videotex terminals as an alternative to computer VDUs. This is further enhanced by the development of gateway facilities by BT in 1982 which allowed videotex terminals to be connected to existing computer systems. Gateways, when linked into telecommunications networks, provide a powerful facility for two-way exchange of information and can extend nationwide and worldwide access to services.

Leading the way in videotex applications is the holiday travel and accommodation business but significant developments have recently featured in the car and freight transport industries and in the banking sector. Currently, the travel business has the single largest population of videotex terminals but a number of the larger industrial organisations, including most of the major car manufacturers, have installed private viewdata systems for dealers/agents and other field sales and engineering personnel, as well as providing a management information service. Developments in banking have included application of videotex for home banking. Hence there is growing use of videotex, particularly in field sales and engineering areas which exploit the low-cost access to corporate databanks through personal computers with Prestel interfaces over the PSTN.

Video

Video conferencing has been used very little in most organisations because of the prohibitive costs of providing a direct service. BT's Confravision service attempted to solve this problem by utilising video circuits nominally installed as a back-up for national distribution of television broadcasts. However, the limited number of studio locations and the problems of travelling to the studios have tended to constrain the take-up of the service. The new BT VideoStream service aims to provide an economic video conferencing service throughout the country and a revived interest amongst potential users. It is expected that video services will have a much greater impact in the future.

Process Control

In many manufacturing organisations and public utilities, on-line process plant control is exercised from Control Centres remote from the plant. In its simplest form (ie telemetry), plant conditions are continuously monitored. In more advanced, continuous-control systems, signals are transmitted to plant actuators to vary the actual operating conditions. Requirements for communications in process control are varied and unique to particular industries; for example, it may be obligatory to operate over dedicated switched lines in real-time to provide the high level of security and performance required in public utilities.

An overall increase in requirements for networks to carry process control information is anticipated, with a move towards greater degrees of centralised control. Actual traffic volumes are likely to diminish as distributed processing techniques continue to develop.

Widespread growth is likely in this type of communications. An influential factor will be the development of energy management and security systems which have many applications, particularly in the retailing market where there is a need to monitor remote business sites.

Personal Computing

The growth of microcomputers creates opportunities for widespread applications of personal computing in areas such as word processing, electronic filing, electronic mailing and database access. Such applications will require occasional but brief connections to networks. Significant use of personal computers as low-cost videotex terminals is also anticipated.

IMPACT ON COMMUNICATIONS SERVICES

The impact of the different types of communications on the communications services provided obviously depends upon the relative volumes (in terms of capacities and requirements) of each type of traffic generated within the organisation.

As an example, based upon the requirements identified in Table 1 and the comments of the preceding section, the following situation might arise:

Voice – most significant today and likely to remain so in future.

Data – significant today but growing fast with large impact in future.

Text – less significant, mainly due to the efficiencies of text transmission, but growing fast and could eventually match data communications in terms of volume.

Video – little use today but greater impact in future and will have substantial demand on communications resources because of high bandwidth requirements and availability at peak times.

Facsimile – large demands for short periods. Could have major impact if greater use results from improved and cheaper products although overnight opportunities could be exploited.

Viewdata, Telex/Teletex, Process Control – low information volume and/or low communication capacity requirements; therefore unlikely to create a major impact.

DAY-TIME	NIGHT-TIME
Voice Data Text Viewdata Telex/Teletex Process Control Video	Facsimile Viewdata Telex/Teletex Process Control Data (limited)

Table 1 Example of Communications Requirements

4 The Next Five Years

INTRODUCTION

In order to plan the communications services which fulfil the type of requirements identified in Chapter 3, it is essential to appreciate the available communications services. Such services include developments in public carrier services and the effects of new technology in the field of communications equipment.

This chapter briefly reviews recent developments in these areas which are most likely to affect the planning of today's corporate communications networks. Likely developments over the next five years are then considered.

CARRIER SERVICES

The British telecommunications network is one of the largest in the world. It is fully automatic and provides a relatively high quality of service. But in common with all other networks in the world it suffers from constraints which inhibit its future development. It is dominated by electromechanical switching equipment which is out-dated, slow in operation, liable to introduce circuit noise, fault prone, and limited in its capability to provide new services.

Technical and economic studies by BT have shown that the most economical way ahead was to modernise the telephone network by the provision of digital exchanges interconnected by digital transmission systems with processor-controlled inter-exchange signalling. The use by BT of digital transmission in networks over shorter distances has been growing for the past fifteen years and more recently this has been coupled with the digitisation of long-distance transmission links and network switching. Digitisation is, therefore, central to the future of telecommunications.

The main internal reason for this digitisation within BT is the prospect of large savings in capital investment. The aim is that this be achieved by the use of new technology, coupled with the opportunities which digital networking offers for the introduction of new services and the integration of all services into a single network.

System X is the key element in BT's plans to modernise its public network. Acceleration and re-orientation of the System X implementation programme now places more emphasis on service for the business user and the completion of the network of main switching units across the UK to cover all key business areas. By 1990, with the completion of the digitisation of the trunk network, System X will allow a rapidly increasing proportion of trunk calls to be routed digitally.

BT, like most other European PTTs, is already investing considerably in the growth of the Integrated Services Digital Network (ISDN). This will provide public switched digital voice and data over one pair of wires to a user's premises. Although widespread introduction of ISDN is some years away, a pilot service opens in June 1984 to provide a means of giving operational experience of voice, text and data integration to BT, manufacturers and users. All System X exchanges installed after mid-1985 will have ISDN capability and BT expect most larger PABXs to move to fully digital interworking with ISDN before 1990.

To meet immediate user needs, in 1981 BT announced the introduction of new digital carriers as the 'X-Stream' family of services. Today the installation of dedicated networks to provide efficient services with faster provision period is well advanced. At the same time a private consortium, Mercury Communications, also announced that they intended to provide a rival public carrier network by late-1983.

Consideration of the capability of the digital network in the provision of other communications requirements resulted in the introduction of the packet switching network in 1981 and the announcement that a text network, Teletex, would be introduced by the mid-eighties. These services are briefly described.

PACKET SWITCHSTREAM (PSS)

PSS, the UK national packet switched data network service, was opened as a pilot service in Autumn 1980 and subsequently on a full commercial basis early in 1981. The aim was to meet the need for better switched data services than can be provided over the PSTN. This service carries data at rates up to 48 Kbit/s and provides users with significant service improvements, including, for example, error checking and protection. Connection to similar data networks in other countries is available via the International Packet Switched Service (IPSS).

The UK PSS network (Figure 4.1), when fully commissioned, will be the most advanced packet switched data service in Europe. Packet switching is now a well accepted data networking technique founded on the use of the internationally implemented X.25 and X.3/28/29 switching protocols.

BT will continue with a substantial expansion of the PSS network to meet growing demands for specialised data services. Inherent in this policy are plans to expand the service to provide 46 packet switching exchanges by 1986, and plans to use new technology to extend and lower the cost of access to the network.

In general, PSS offers no major cost advantage over private data networks for the large data user, but for those organisations which have specific requirements for switching low volumes of data, PSS is often an attractive proposition. PSS has a number of significant operational advantages which can be most easily exploited when customer networks are suitably configured. As a result BT expect to see PSS become a focus for services that are application-specific, and also for links between private and public networks through inter-network gateways. Gateways between networks are expected to lead to a growth in electronic message services using Teletex protocols. An example is InterStream One which is the first gateway to allow full interconnection between terminals on the PSS and telex networks. Later, an interworking facility — InterStream Three — for terminals on PSTN, PSS and telex will be provided specifically for the Teletex service.

Leased circuits have in the past formed the backbone of corporate networks because of the shortcomings of PSTN; for example,

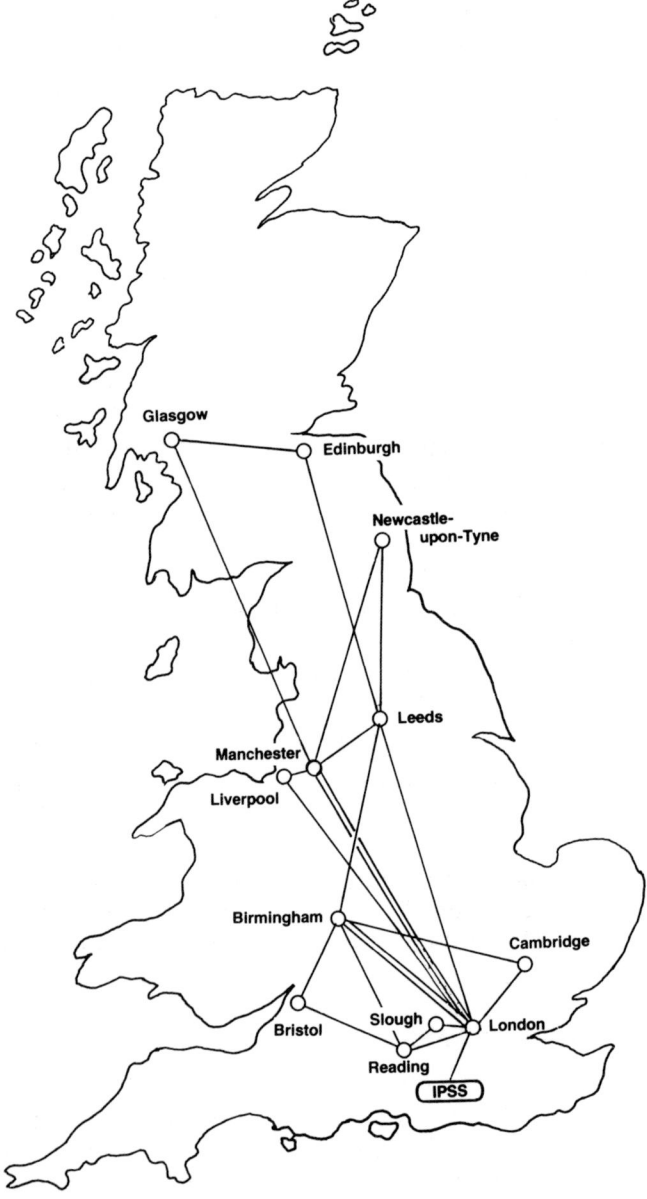

Figure 4.1 PSS Network

call set-up times in the case of voice networks, reliability (eg bit error rates) in the case of data networks, and cost reasons in terms of call charges. PSS is the first public network offering a level of service comparable with that of private networks; for example, security and on-line access to billing information. ISDN will offer further advantages in the future. Such developments suggest a swing towards public networks.

INTEGRATED DIGITAL ACCESS (IDA)

The ISDN, referred to earlier, will provide fast 'circuit switched' services and access over a common access link – marketed as Integrated Digital Access (IDA) – to a range of other network services. The ISDN will ultimately provide an all-purpose digital switching network capable of dealing with all forms of communications traffic (ie voice, data and text). Interconnection of nodes within the network will be through optical fibres and switching will be effected by the new System X exchanges when such exchanges are installed. The completion of the all-purpose data digital switching network will not effectively be achieved until the beginning of the next century. However, BT intend to achieve the connection of all major cities by the end of this decade. There are already over 100,000 miles of digital transmission systems in the BT network, with an additional 100,000 miles to be added every year.

Digital trunk transmission systems are now being introduced, operating at 8 Mbit/s, 34 Mbit/s, 120 Mbit/s and 140 Mbit/s, using balanced pair and coaxial copper cable, optical fibre cable and microwave radio bearers. Figure 4.2 shows the 1983 position; by 1988, sixty-one System X digital main network exchanges will be in service, and by 1990 the trunk digital transmission network will be complete.

X-STREAM SERVICES

To meet immediate needs, BT is already well advanced in the installation of dedicated networks. With most of the principal cities now digitally linked, a leased private service is now available upon which a digital private network can be based. Three private services are available with the X-Stream family: MegaStream, KiloStream and SatStream.

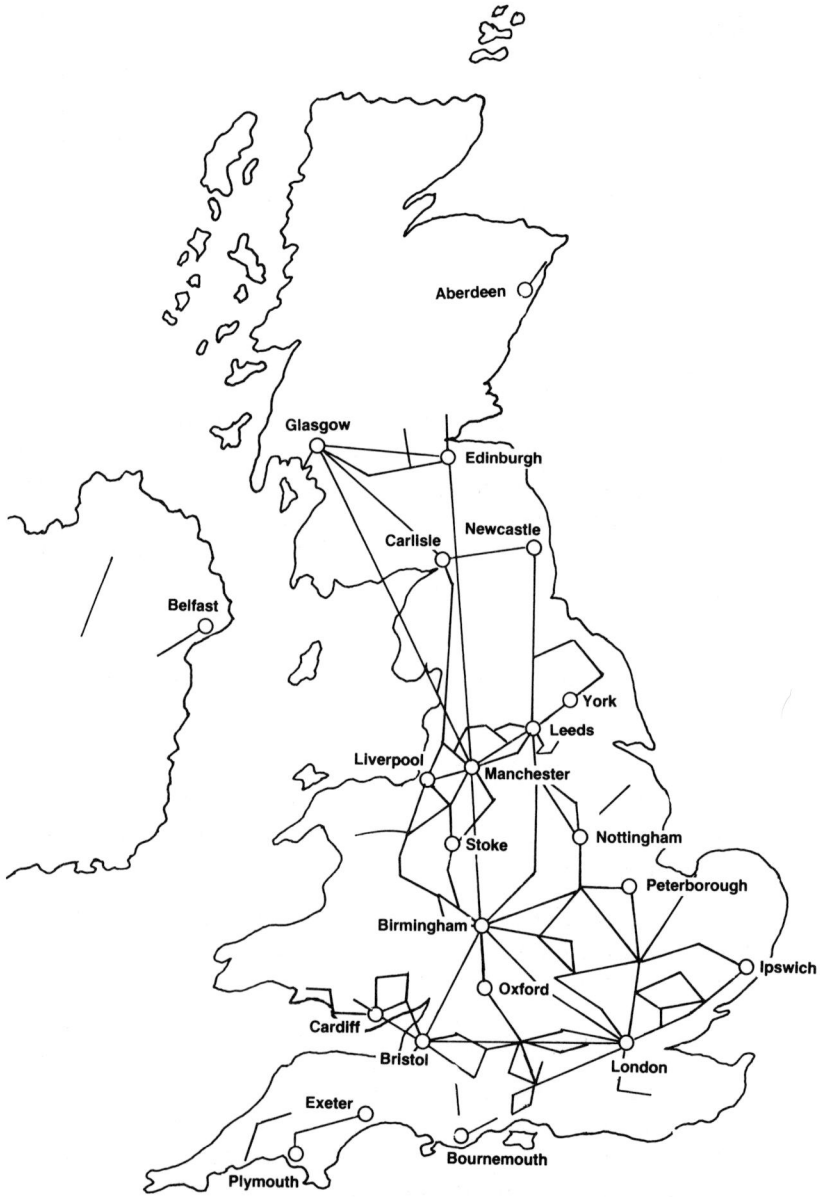

Figure 4.2   X-Stream Network

MegaStream

The MegaStream service, which was first connected at the end of 1982, is a high-capacity, digital private circuit service, which can be specially engineered at speeds of 2, 8, 34 or 140 Mbit/s and can be used for very high speed data links or to provide links between digital PABXs. Presentation to a customer's premises will be in one of three forms:

— optical fibre;

— dish-to-dish communication;

— traditional copper network.

A 2 Mbit/s link can carry up to 30 voice channels at 64 Kbit/s. Channels can be multiplexed to give the combination of voice and data to suit specific requirements as shown in Figure 4.3. Typical termination of this service in user premises will be to a multiplexer which will subdivide the circuit into 30 tributaries, each with a data rate of 64 Kbit/s and providing the following alternatives:

— voice channel at 64 Kbit/s;

— two voice channels using data compression techniques at 32 Kbit/s;

— digital data channel at 64 Kbit/s.

By using sub-multiplexing techniques the digital bandwidth of 64 Kbit/s can be subdivided further to carry a mix of voice, data and text simultaneously.

Multiplexers are offered by a number of suppliers and by BT in the guise of MegaStream 2 multiplexer services. It is worth indicating the developments in this area:

— initial development to provide 30 analogue channels derived from the 2 Mbit/s service. This service became available in London in September 1981 under the special 'London Overlay' scheme; primarily designed for the transmission of speech, such a service requires the use of modems for digital attachments;

— next development to provide 6 × 64 Kbit/s 'tributaries' and 24 analogue channels derived from one 2 Mbit/s service

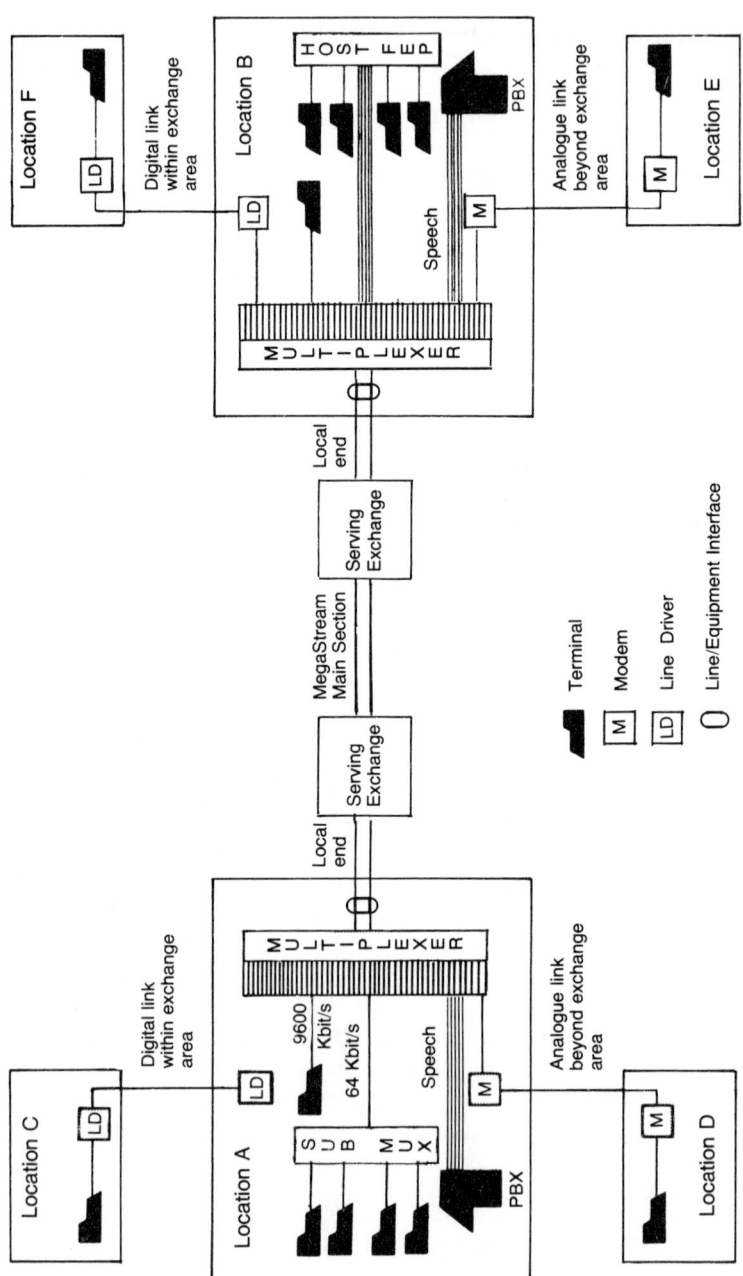

Figure 4.3 MegaStream Circuit with Multiplexers

with each digital tributary offering an X.21 or X.21 bis interface. This service became available in late-1982 under the London Overlay scheme, and will be available elsewhere as the national network develops;

— further development to provide unstructured channels at 64 Kbit/s or structured channels at internationally agreed rates;

— final development to offer a wholly digital transmission capability providing 30 digital unstructured tributaries each offering an X.21 interface. This service became available in 1983.

MegaStream is therefore aimed at providing backbone links for large organisations' corporate networks whether it be through the linking of PABXs (with both analogue and digital presentations), the linking of large computers through multiplexed structured channels, or the provision of high-speed point-to-point data services.

MegaStream is more economic than FDM widebands for all voice-plus-data links and for most voice-only links. BT therefore expect that the use of MegaStream will increase rapidly, replacing all FDM wideband circuits before the end of the decade.

Typical cost comparisons carried out since the announcement of X-Stream services indicate that the typical cost of a MegaStream connection providing a minimum of 30 high-grade channels is equivalent to the cost of ten traditional tariff T circuits. Costs for MegaStream are obviously dependent upon the form of presentation adopted, (ie multiplexed or line connected) and the serving options appropriate to the customer's site (eg screen cable, polyquad cable, optical fibre, microwave, radio). In all cases MegaStream services require special cabling from user premises to the exchange. This requirement is reflected in the tariffs which show a substantial sum for the first circuit with subsequent incremental costs considerably less.

For organisations with large communications requirements very substantial savings can therefore be achieved by the replacement of existing FDM links and the provision of new links by high-speed MegaStream connections.

KiloStream

For companies who require single channel access to digital services, BT is offering the KiloStream services. KiloStream provides a range of point-to-point digital private services which are particularly suitable for smaller organisations with smaller communications requirements. KiloStream will also form a logical and necessary part of networks for larger organisations serving smaller locations.

KiloStream service is provided via BT's nationwide private circuit digital network which is also the basis for the MegaStream services. As shown in Figure 4.4, KiloStream is a dedicated national network which utilises digital network plant to provide a 64 Kbit/s facility from which recognised data rates are derived. Full synchronous duplex transmission at 2400, 4800, 9600, 48000, or 64000 bit/s is offered.

KiloStream service is provided on a point-to-point basis, giving end-to-end digital transmission between customer addresses. An integral part of the service is the Network Terminating Unit (NTU) provided at each end of the circuit. The NTU provides the CCITT interface (X.21, X.21 bis) to suit the attached device, terminates the 4-wire circuit connection, and returns diagnostic control signals to the network. At transmission speeds up to 48 Kbit/s the KiloStream service is structured by the addition of two supervisory bits to each six bits of data transmitted by the user. These supervisory bits which are added, transparently to the user, by the NTU are used for monitoring and control purposes in the network and then automatically removed by the NTU at the destination address. This enables BT to carry out in-service monitoring and fault condition diagnosis at its two X-Stream Service Centres located in London and Manchester. Unstructured KiloStream is available when the full 64 Kbit/s service is required but at this rate a reduced level of fault diagnostics is provided and, unlike the structured services, no in-service monitoring is available.

KiloStream is primarily a data transmission service, offering standard transmission rates and CCITT interfaces, which is particularly suited to various data applications and to providing digital local ends to private digital networks. But KiloStream will also carry private circuits used for voice traffic, using 64 or 32 Kbit/s

THE NEXT FIVE YEARS

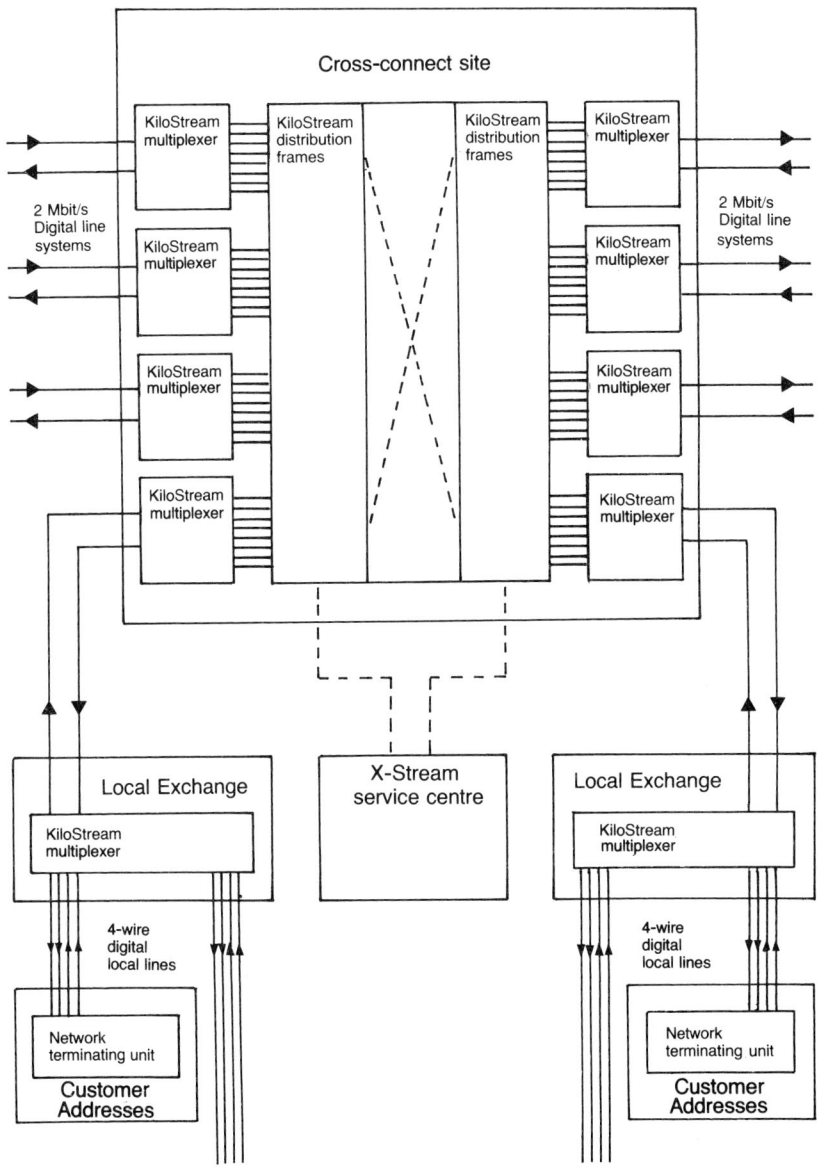

Figure 4.4 KiloStream Network

digital encoding. The service will progressively extend throughout the UK from mid-1983 to provide virtually national coverage by 1986. This will enable BT to replace analogue Datel private circuits used for data by digital private circuits. At the same time it is expected that the majority of new long-distance voice private circuits will be provided over this network.

The use of encoded voice at 32 Kbit/s enables voice, data and signalling to be carried over a single KiloStream circuit and hence speeds the development of integrated networks by allowing users to build mixed voice/data networks.

Sub-64 Kbit/s data channels can be time division multiplexed onto the 64 Kbit/s circuit using bit interleaved time division multiplexers available from BT and other suppliers. Such a device accepts multiple voice and low-speed synchronous, asynchronous or isochronous inputs and multiplexes them by interleaving their data bits into a single aggregate output rate.

A new range of multiplexers is available from BT for the KiloStream and MegaStream services to facilitate the multiplexing of the various channels to 64 Kbit/s and 2.048 Mbit/s (MegaStream). Typically, the NETMUX K12 TDM provides up to 12 channels maximum with data rates from 150 bit/s to 32 Kbit/s (up to seven mixed channel rates simultaneously) and a voice channel. The aggregate data is designed to interface into the 64 Kbit/s service and interfaces are available for V24, V10, V11 and V35 (48 Kbit/s). The voice channel uses 32 or 28.8 Kbit/s of the aggregate and presents an interface in terms of level, impedance, etc equivalent to that of a voice carrier channel, plus the ability to accept in-band signalling. A speech codec tributary card with in-band signalling, to enable voice services to be carried as part of KiloStream, is also under development.

KiloStream is competitive in cost terms, compared with analogue circuits with modems, at all data rates and over all but the shortest distances. For example (charges for 1/1/83):

	Rental
160 Km tariff T circuit with 9600 bit/s modems –	£6,420
160 Km KiloStream 9600 bit/s service –	£2,800

At higher data rates such as 48 Kbit/s, KiloStream is substantially cheaper than Datel 48K using modems and specially provided FDM wideband circuits, for example:

	Connection	Rental
142 Km FDM wideband	– £26,000	£15,00
142 Km KiloStream	– £400	£3,710

SatStream

The last of the present range of X-Stream services will be SatStream which provides for communications via satellites. SatStream is the private small dish satellite service which opens in mid-1984 and which will cover most of Western Europe; it will be based on the European Communications Satellite and the French Telecom 1 satellite systems. Satellite communications direct from small dish aerials mounted on, or close to, user premises will form an integral part of BT's network marketing strategy. In addition to its service to Europe, SatStream will also, for example, provide the opportunity for links within the UK for point-to-multipoint broadcast transmission, high capacity temporary and emergency links, and links for users located in remote sites (eg oil rigs) that are difficult to serve terrestrially .

In international services, BT are committed to the expansion of both satellite and cable systems with a major stake in a North Atlantic optical fibre cable planned for 1988. BT also have a major share in IntelSat.

MERCURY COMMUNICATIONS

In 1982 a consortium consisting of Cable and Wireless, Barclays Merchant Bank and British Petroleum was granted a licence to provide an alternative public carrier service alongside British Telecom. This network, known as Mercury, will provide by the end of 1984 a communications link connecting major commercial centres. The Mercury 'figure of eight' network (Figure 4.5) will consist of optical fibres laid in ducts alongside British Rail tracks with links to user premises via microwave radio links.

Basic connection is a 64 Kbit/s circuit, through which can be sent one voice channel (PCM coded) or a combination of voice (coded

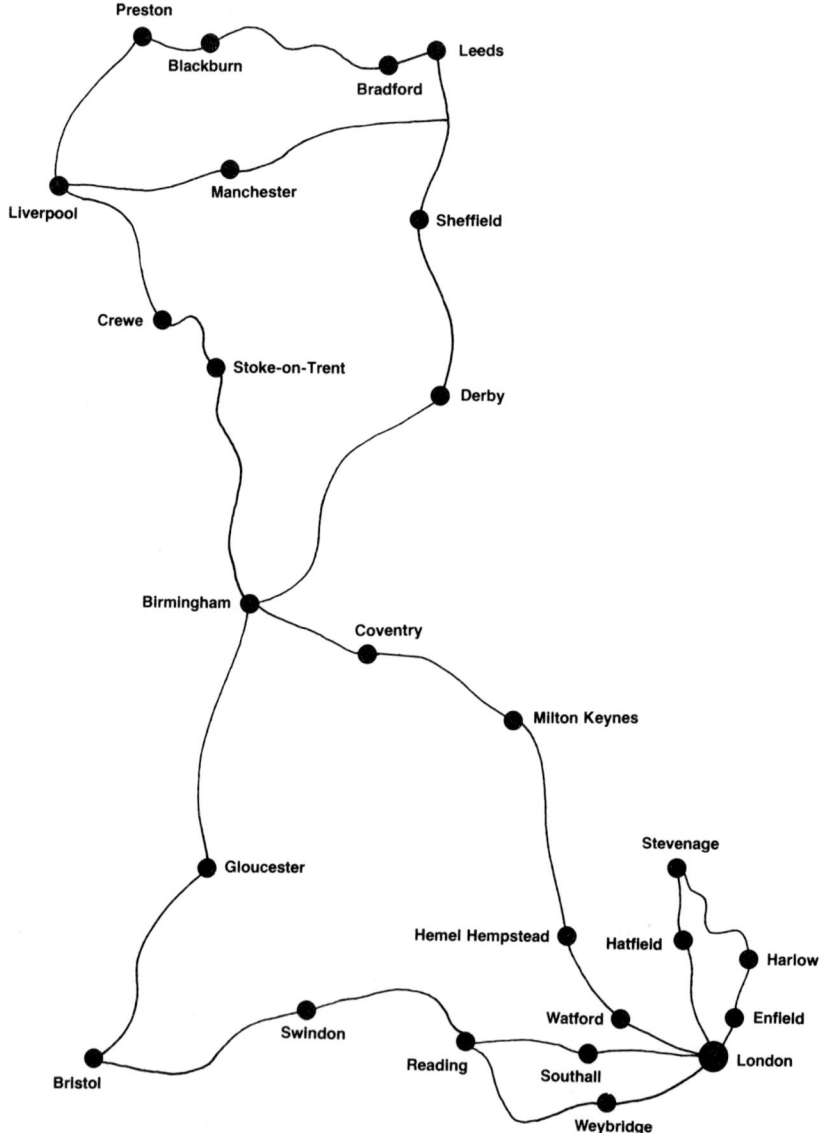

Figure 4.5 Mercury Network

in 32 Kbit/s) together with data circuits to a total aggregate of 30 Kbit/s, or data circuits up to an aggregate of 64 Kbit/s and with synchronous and asynchronous interfaces. For large organisations with private networks, a 2 Mbit/s service offers either 30 voice channels or a combination of voice channels and 64 Kbit/s data ports.

The services which can be carried by these circuits range from voice through low-speed data to computer-to-computer interfaces and video conferencing. When switching is introduced into the network, circuits will be switched at the CCITT standard rate of 64 Kbit/s, using high-speed digital switches.

The Mercury optical fibre cable trunk network is being constructed with a ready-for-service date of September 1984 for phases embracing London to Birmingham, Birmingham to Leeds, Leeds to Manchester and London to Swindon. Subsequent phases of the network are planned to be implemented later.

In the meantime, a 34 Mbit/s microwave route is being established from London through Birmingham to Manchester to connect the local radio networks in these centres to that of London. A digital microwave radio network provides a point-to-multipoint service in London and is already transmitting (May 1983).

Mercury has applied for permission to place an IntelSat earth station in London to provide a leased line facility to the United States. Further international links will be established in the future by the addition of earth stations working to Europe, the Middle East and Far East.

The Mercury network is designed to carry all forms of digital services and is designed to permit the introduction of digital switched services. This enables any node in the network to be converted into a digital switching centre, capable of handling any form of 64 Kbit/s based service which may emerge in the future as a result of the ISDN concept.

TELEX/TELETEX

The 1980s will see a continued investment by BT in the development and maintenance of existing switched services. Telex is an example of a mature network for which BT see growth. The network will be comprehensively modernised with SPC exchanges during 1985 to provide a wide range of extra facilities.

Teletex is the new British Telecom advanced text communication service to be provided during the course of 1984 and beyond. Teletex will not be a new and discrete network but a combination of the Public Switched Telephone Network (PSTN), the existing telex network and Packet SwitchStream.

The connection from terminal equipment into the Teletex network will be via an equipment interface conforming to CCITT standards and as such it will allow a full interconnect ability for all terminal equipment meeting such recommendations. A major advantage of the new services is that communication between devices of different speeds will be achieved.

In this way a word processor transmitting at, say, 2400 bits per second will be able to link with a telex machine operating at only 50 bits per second, the buffering facilities being provided at the local Teletex exchanges. The protocol conversion necessary to enable devices to talk to each other will again be offered by the public exchange. Standards of presentation and character set will be uniform and a directory will be published as for telex.

The development of 'message switches' provides the ability to input and print information at much faster speeds than the telex network is capable of (ie 50 bits per second). Intercommunication between such switches can therefore be carried out at speeds such as 2400 bits per second or faster. The message switch equipment is also capable of providing the buffering and storage facilities necessary to receive the information at 2400 bits per second and transmit it onto the public network at the speed of 50 bits per second.

Specialised systems (for example, in banking environments) have been developed and have enabled major cost reductions to be achieved by reduction in the number of telex operating staff and faster provision of information. However, the development of telex services is still restricted by the need to employ some form of messenger service within organisations to achieve the final distribution of the message.

Recent developments in PABXs have included the ability for the basic telephone to be extended to form a multi-purpose work-

THE NEXT FIVE YEARS

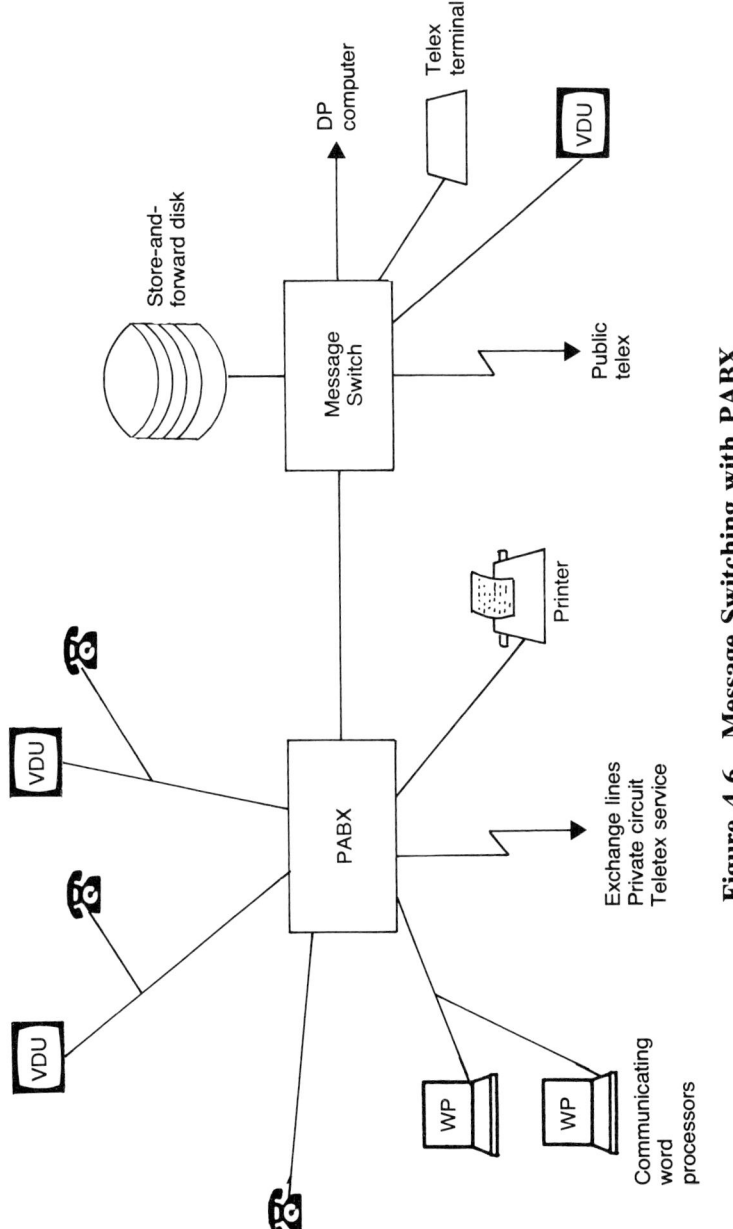

Figure 4.6 Message Switching with PABX

station. Such devices typically include the use of VDUs and keyboards together with some form of simple line printer and local processing and printing capability. The development of the message switch by the major suppliers has therefore radically changed in that they are now considering the interconnection of message switches with the PABX (Figure 4.6) to provide faster distribution of messages, more effective use of services and direct composition of telex messages by the end-user. It is anticipated that within the next two years there will be a major increase in installed systems of this type offering significant advantages to the user.

The use of multi-purpose workstations is not limited to preparing and receiving messages. They can also be used, depending on their inherent capability, for access to local/remote computer files and remote data banks, local computing facilities, and for management of electronic mail and filing. In such applications the role of the message switches or associated PABXs is usually limited to providing some form of communication protocol conversion.

CONFERENCING

Until recently, conferencing facilities have been either the video conferencing facilities supplied by British Telecom, or more typically the simple teleconferencing facilities available on many PABXs. As such, they have been relatively primitive.

The video conferencing services available from British Telecom (Confravision), although providing good and effective communication, have few studios available for such conferences; thus users need to travel. Many organisations feel that if travelling is required to a video conference studio then an extended journey to their own offices usually provides more effective utilisation of time and more successful conferences and meetings.

PABX teleconference facilities have equally been unsuccessful. The reason for this is that a multi-user conference on a simple telephone of only 3400 hertz bandwidth has meant that the conversation must be in a simplex mode, ie in one direction at one time. In practice there is usually continual contention by conference members to take the line which results in a noticeable degradation of recognisable speech.

Developments in audio-teleconferencing and more recently video conferencing have provided much improved facilities. An audio-teleconferencing facility is provided by BT's Orator system. Terminals are set up at the user's premises with connections via two exchange lines rather than a single line, allowing conversations in a duplex mode rather than the simplex mode. Such equipment is relatively inexpensive and has enabled many organisations to achieve effective savings.

The concept of telephone with pictures is well established but has always floundered on the problems of transmission technology which has proved prohibitively expensive, particularly for service direct to the user's own premises. Recent developments in video conferencing resulted in the announcement of a new BT service (VideoStream) during 1983. VideoStream utilises digital technology. Encoding equipment compresses full motion colour or monochrome video signals into the digital equivalent of only 30 telephone channels. This new technology combined with digital transmission services and digital switching capabilities means that VideoStream can be provided throughout the country. Video conference services are possible not only to other VideoStream users but also to BT public studios and video conferencing users overseas. In addition to a switched service, a point-to-point service can be provided over the MegaStream network.

During 1983 BT provided a number of larger organisations with video conferencing to their own premises as part of a 'Visual Services Trial'. The trial phase is to be followed by the full VideoStream service.

The application of good conferencing facilities such as those now emerging and described above will therefore allow considerable reductions in travelling in the future. This will result in improved costs and increased productivity.

5 Options for the Future

INTRODUCTION

Advances in semiconductor technology and economic pressures have led to the increasing use of digital techniques in public telephone networks. Today digital techniques are being used not only in inter-exchange transmission but also in subscriber loops by incorporating analogue-to-digital converters into telephone handsets. We may expect the public telephone networks of today to evolve into the end-to-end digital networks of tomorrow. In practice, pulse code modulation (PCM) techniques are being used to convert analogue telephone channels into digital channels with a bit rate of 64 Kbit/s. However, end-to-end digitisation allows the standard 64 Kbit/s channels employed throughout digital telephone networks to be used not only for PCM encoded speech but also for a wide range of new and existing non-voice services. This leads to the concept of an Integrated Services Digital Network (ISDN).

INTEGRATED SERVICES DIGITAL NETWORK (ISDN)

The concept emerging for the basic user access to the ISDN is shown in Figure 5.1 which illustrates the functional structure and the related interfaces at the user's premises and at the digital local exchange. Due to the larger data rates which result from the use of digital technology, a time division multiplexed channel structure of two B-channels and one D-channel is made available at the ISDN user/network interface via existing two-wire subscriber links.

B designates one of two independent circuit switched 64 Kbit/s

52 CORPORATE COMMUNICATIONS NETWORKS

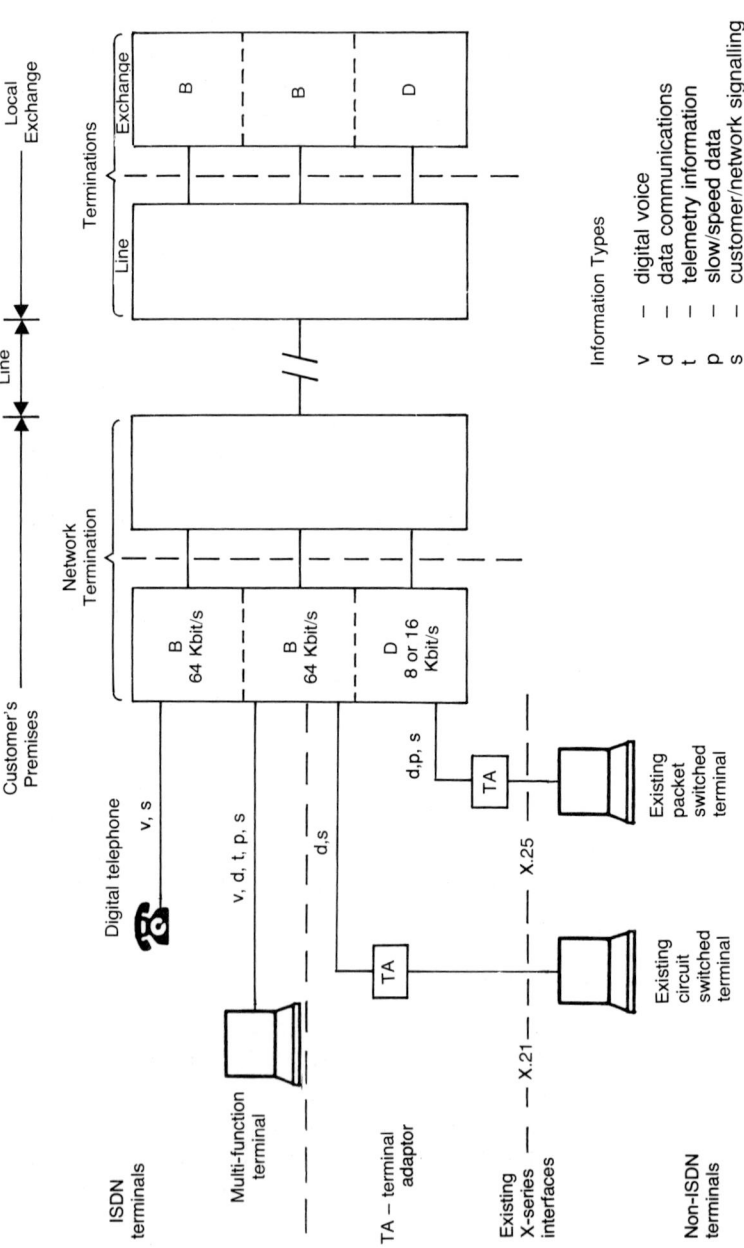

Figure 5.1 ISDN User Access

user information channels which can be used simultaneously to different addresses. The standard bit rate of 64 Kbit/s derives from the situation where digital transmission and switching systems are based on 64 Kbit/s PCM channels as described in CCITT Recommendation G.703. The B-channels are characterised by end-to-end transparency and, as well as carrying out their original task of transporting PCM encoded digital voice, can also be used for the transport of data information, or other types of non-voice information such as text, facsimile, video, etc.

D designates a separate signalling channel which is shared in multi-terminal installations by the set of terminals which may be attached to the particular ISDN network. Although the access configuration is shown typically in Figure 5.1 as star connected, both bus and ring intra-site distribution networks can be foreseen. The D-channel is message interleaved, being primarily designed to carry the signalling information which controls the handling of B-channels through the ISDN. Enhanced signalling capabilities are offered to ISDN services because the transfer of user and network signalling information does not interfere with the transport of user data on the B-channels. In addition to carrying signalling information, the D-channel might optionally be used for the transport of slow-speed data and for telemetry information.

This latter category includes new services such as remote meter reading, telecontrol, remote alarm monitoring, etc. The use of the D-channel for slow-speed data, however, will be limited in terms of data throughput and quality of service, if significant performance penalties for the prime task of the D-channel (ie the carriage of signalling information) are to be avoided.

ISDN USER INTERFACES

New ISDN terminals will use a new universal interface which is designed to the ISDN channel structure and employs common channel signalling. In effect this interface can be regarded as a service-independent 'ISDN-type' interface to which voice terminals as well as non-voice terminals can be directly connected. A call control procedure is used which is common to all circuit switched ISDN services, ie digital telephony and circuit switched data communications. ISDN terminals will be offered with multifunction and multiservice capabilities to exploit the full range of features provided by ISDN.

With the current availability of both circuit and packet switched services on dedicated data networks in accordance with adopted X-series CCITT recommendations, provisions have to be made for the connection of existing text and data terminal equipment to the ISDN. This requires existing X-series interfaces, such as X.21 and X.25 corresponding to circuit and packet switched services respectively, at bit rates lower than 64 Kbit/s according to recommendation X.1. Terminals with interfaces X.21 or X.25 will be connected to the ISDN network by means of suitable data rate adaptors which primarily adapt the X.1 user rates to the 64 Kbit/s bearer rate of the B-channel.

Whilst X.21 can be completely integrated into ISDN, the provision of packet switched services with interface X.25 can be expected to have a greater impact on a circuit switched network like ISDN. Nevertheless a need for offering X.25 data communication services to ISDN users is anticipated and expected to continue after extensive introduction of circuit switched ISDN data communication services. This is due to the particular advantages of packet switching for interactive application, ie bursty traffic (eg low-volume users with long connect times) and for the multichannel access features of recommendation X.25.

VOICE/DATA INTEGRATION OPPORTUNITIES

Organisations typically operate separate voice and data networks as a means of meeting their present-day communications requirements. These networks consist of a wide range of shared and dedicated facilities for voice and data and have traditionally been planned, designed, operated and managed as completely separated entities within the organisation.

Whilst voice services are based on a single telecommunication application (ie the switching and transmission of a 4 KHz signal with well defined characteristics), data services are required to accommodate a wide range of applications. In contrast to voice signals, data signals also require considerably improved error performance, are generally bursty in nature, and have application-dependent delay and throughput requirements.

While voice networks are being used for voiceband applications, economics and functional requirements have traditionally dictated a need to establish separate data networks. Data communications has tended to have grown out of the central mainframe world to meet a growing demand for remote terminals and distributed processing, and has developed mainly through data processing's own efforts because data services were not available from the PTTs and other carriers. In large organisations a number of data networks will have been required to meet the overall data communications requirement.

Over the last few decades, very significant developments have taken place in the provision of national and worldwide voice services. Today stored program control, digital switching and transmission, and enhanced signalling systems are being used. At the same time technology associated with data communications has moved very rapidly to suit the needs of the dp environment with the development of packet switching, intelligent multiplexers, terminals and modems.

Within the user environment two trends can be identified as organisations attempt to increase the usefulness yet at the same time contain and perhaps decrease the costs of their networks:

— large organisations are integrating their several application-specific data networks as a means of containing network costs, increasing network utilisation, developing increased functions of terminals and enhancing the capability of central network management and operation;

— both large and small organisations are looking at the total integration of their voice and data networks, motivated by a need to permit data services to benefit from the economies of scale previously only inherent in the voice network, and as a central strategy to develop a transport mechanism aimed at increasing office productivity.

In practice, what opportunities are associated with the integration of voice and data networks? Let us first consider the operational requirements of each form of communication.

Voice and Data Requirements

Voice and data services can be considered as call-based, transaction-based, store-and-forward, or broadcast and conference. Of these, voice and data services have the greatest degree of commonality in the area of call-based services. With the significant developments of the last few years voice systems have become rich with features, eg call transfer, auto dialling, direct inward dialling, etc. A comparison of features found in both voice and data systems shows that many of these features are common to both.

In addition to the commonality of features for separate voice and data applications, current voice and data conversion techniques make possible the integration of voice and data into a single application in which voice signals are digitised, processed, stored and retrieved. Examples to be found today include voice mail and dictation. In the future when speech recognition techniques attain higher quality of output at low cost a new set of voice and data interactive applications can be envisaged.

Network management is the range of activities required to plan, organise, control, maintain and evolve a network at optimum cost and performance. In many organisations this function is currently split between the telecommunications department (for voice) and the computer centre (for data). However, a review of voice and data network requirements indicates that the basic philosophies and techniques used in operating voice and data networks are fundamentally the same. This degree of commonality will become even higher in the future with the emergence of technology integration which will allow both voice and data applications to be provided by the same extension set, transmission medium and serving equipment. Differences between various networks and voice and data applications will be masked out, thereby presenting the opportunity to combine the two separate network management capabilities into a single cost-effective function.

Hence the basic premise of voice and data integration is realised through the provision of the common requirements in the same networking system. This is made possible by the emerging technology integration opportunities; but what are these opportunities today? In particular, what opportunities are provided in transmission technology, network switching and network interfacing and signalling?

Transmission Technologies – Trends

The public telephone network is based on the multiplexing of 64 Kbit/s PCM channels. In the future more efficient coding schemes, for example at 32 Kbit/s, will be used. Data transmission can be accomplished by rate adaption to the 64 Kbit/s channels which are becoming increasingly available in the public telephone network. Alternatively sub-64 Kbit/s data channels can be multiplexed into the 64 Kbit/s channels using bit interleaved time division multiplexing techniques.

Inter-site digital transmission systems are used to carry both voice and data traffic. The implementation of data services on the digital voice network requires the upgrading of performance characteristics. This is usually achieved by the use of high-performance trunks, separate trunk groups or the use of error correction and control techniques.

Local transmission systems for accessing the digital trunk network can likewise be designed to carry voice and data traffic. In order to exploit the existing one cable pair per customer in the UK local telephone network, it is necessary to develop a transmission system which will transmit 64 Kbit/s plus a signalling channel and an auxiliary low bit rate channel. This is the basis of the ISDN system described earlier.

Operation over the 2-wire line requires duplex working using either burst mode or echo cancelling techniques. In burst mode the two directions of transmission are separated in time, and bursts of data (10 bits) are transmitted at a high rate (256 Kbit/s) in one direction and then the other. More recently, echo cancellation has emerged as an alternative to burst mode for local network applications. In echo cancelling systems, signals for both directions of transmission are transmitted simultaneously, thereby minimising the bandwidth wasted in burst mode operation. Both types of transmission are being developed for BT's pilot ISDN service.

Network Switching Technologies – Trends

Switching of voice is normally achieved via circuit switching although packet switching may eventually become cost-effective for applications such as transcontinental links.

Switching of data on the other hand can be achieved by circuit, packet and message switching. The choice of technique to be used for a particular application is very much dependent upon the traffic requirements and delay requirements associated with the application. In general, circuit switching is not as cost-effective as packet switching for bursty and low-speed data traffic.

However, circuit switching with sub-64 Kbit/s paths increases the efficiency of handling voice and data traffic. In order to accommodate a wide range of applications it is likely that both circuit and packet switching techniques will continue to be used in response to the challenge of voice and data integration.

Interfacing and Signalling – Trends

The data communications user and industry are faced with a large number of different data protocols and interfaces which results in high costs of development, provision and maintenance. In packet switching this is achieved by the use of the widely accepted X.25 data link and network level protocols. However, at the physical level a large number of both voice and data interface standards exist.

These present-day voice and data standards are not suited to meet the emerging need for an integrated voice/data user/network interface. Therefore, CCITT as part of its work on ISDN is defining a family of interfaces. CCITT is also studying a multichannel ISDN interface for use by PABXs and communications controllers.

The conventional in-band telephony signalling system with information and control signals sharing the same transmission bandwidth creates significant limitations to the accommodation of new services and advanced features. To overcome these limitations, CCITT has developed the common channel signalling Number 7 system in which the control signals known as 'user parts' are transmitted over high-speed signalling links physically separated from the information channels. It has a wide variety of control signals to accommodate existing and future services. Common channel signalling is an important element in BT/Mercury plans to efficiently handle voice and data circuit switched services in the integrated digital network.

Clearly the opportunities for integration will exist in the technology of the future but what is the current state of developments in the UK?

CURRENT DEVELOPMENTS (VOICE/DATA)
National Digital Private Circuit Network

An important division in current communications services is between switched networks and leased circuit facilities. Historically, leased circuits have been preferred as a basis for private networks on cost and performance criteria. Despite the expected increase in the attractiveness of switched networks referred to earlier, it is recognised that leased circuit facilities will continue to form a major part of private networks in the future.

As discussed in Chapter 4, BT has adopted a strategy for the provision of a network resource which makes available high-quality digital private circuits to the user. This network resource is the National Digital Private Circuit Network (NDPCN).

NDPCN is structurally part of BT's digital main network (Integrated Digital Network, IDN), but is functionally separate and organised to overcome a number of the long-standing problems common in leased circuit provision. For example, in NDPCN the main network portions of a customer's circuits are drawn from pre-provided main network links, thereby speeding up lead times.

The basic structure of the NDPCN is shown in Figure 5.2. The nodes of the network are cross-connect sites in central BT exchanges which are linked by digital line systems. From these central cross-connect sites digital line systems radiate to additional multiplexer sites. Digital transmission to the customer is normally implemented over existing cable pairs at 64 Kbit/s, but also by specially prepared screened cable, optical fibre or radio systems.

NDPCN is the basis for the MegaStream and KiloStream services outlined in Chapter 4. BT's strategy for the provision and development of the network allows further services to be configured. From 1984, NDPCN facilities will be linked into the ISDN pilot network (described in the following section) to enable the development of a full spectrum of network transmission services.

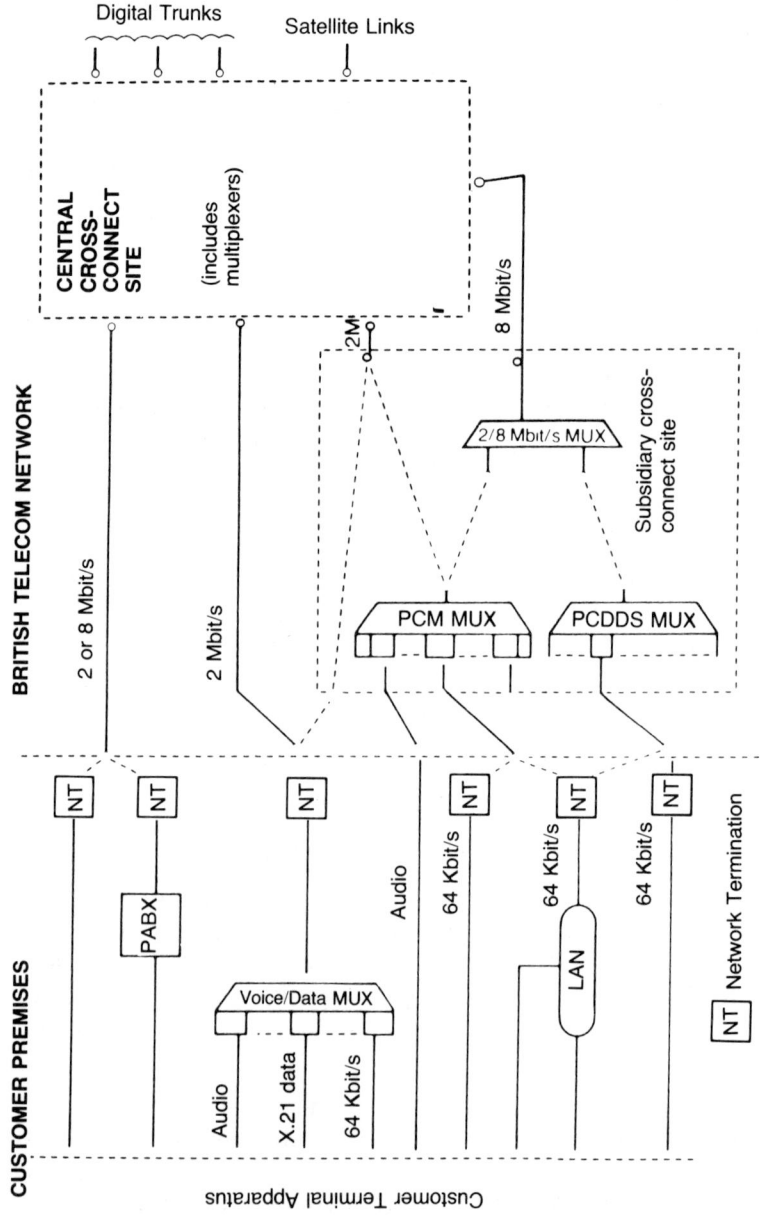

Figure 5.2 Digital Private Circuit Network (DPCN)

ISDN in the UK

By the third quarter of 1984, BT will have brought into service the initial installations of its Integrated Services Digital Network (ISDN). As described earlier, this network will provide users with a variety of new services and facilities, many of which are made possible by the increased bandwidth provided by a wholly digital connection; for example, circuit switched data at rates up to 64 Kbit/s, multiplexed (30 × 64 Kbit/s) interface to digital PABXs, and message-based signalling system.

IDA (Integrated Digital Access) is the user's link with the ISDN, via his local System X exchange. IDA gives access over a single link to many BT services. It combines voice and data transmission over this single digital link and thereby replaces the need for separate access to each existing BT network. BT's initial IDA service (Pilot Service) is described below.

IDA Pilot Service

Each ISDN user is supplied with either an 80 Kbit/s or a 2048 Kbit/s digital link between his premises and the ISDN local exchange as shown in Figure 5.3. The 80 Kbit/s (single line) connection provides the following full-duplex channels over the link using existing BT local cables:

— a 64 Kbit/s primary channel (B channel);

— an 8 Kbit/s secondary channel (B' channel);

— an 8 Kbit/s signalling channel (D channel).

The primary channel (B channel) is capable of supporting all CCITT X.1 synchronous data rates, ie 2400 bit/s, 4800 bit/s, 9600 bit/s and 48 Kbit/s, as well as synchronous data at the additional rates of 64 Kbit/s and 8 Kbit/s. This channel is also used for voice communications using network-compatible A-law PCM encoding.

The secondary channel (B' channel) is used for carrying data at X.1 synchronous rates of 2400 and 4800 bit/s, asynchronous data sampled at 8 KHz, and 8 Kbit/s synchronous data. The secondary channel of 8 Kbit/s is reiterated at the exchange to form a 64 Kbit/s data stream which can be switched in the normal manner through the network.

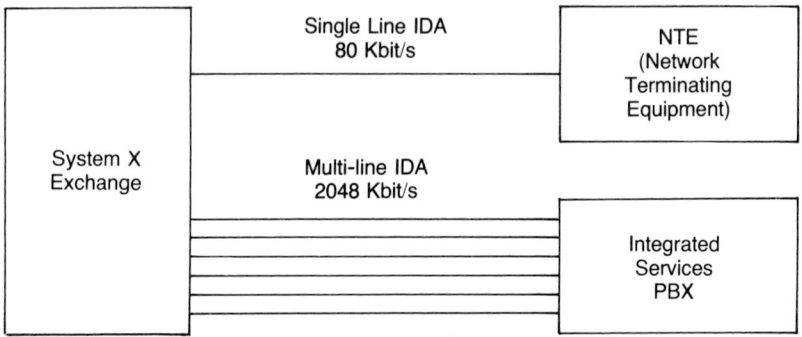

Figure 5.3   IDA Pilot Service

Data interfaces to CCITT recommendations X.21 (switched and leased circuit operation) and X.21 bis are supported. Where user data rates are less than the digit rate of the channel then status information is also conveyed.

User access to these channels is via a Network Terminating Equipment (NTE) which provides the interface with the user's terminal equipment and carries out call control and line transmission termination functions (see Figure 5.4). The rate adaptor converts between the lower data rates and that of the access channel (64 or 8 Kbit/s). For the initial phase of ISDN service two NTEs will be available.

NTE1 includes a digital telephone, keypad, display, and a data port capable of operating at up to 64 Kbit/s using an X.21 bis interface.

NTE3 comprises a wall-mounted remote unit providing up to six data port connections selected from a range which currently includes:

— X.21 and X.21 bis;

— 2-wire analogue;

— MODEC.

OPTIONS FOR THE FUTURE

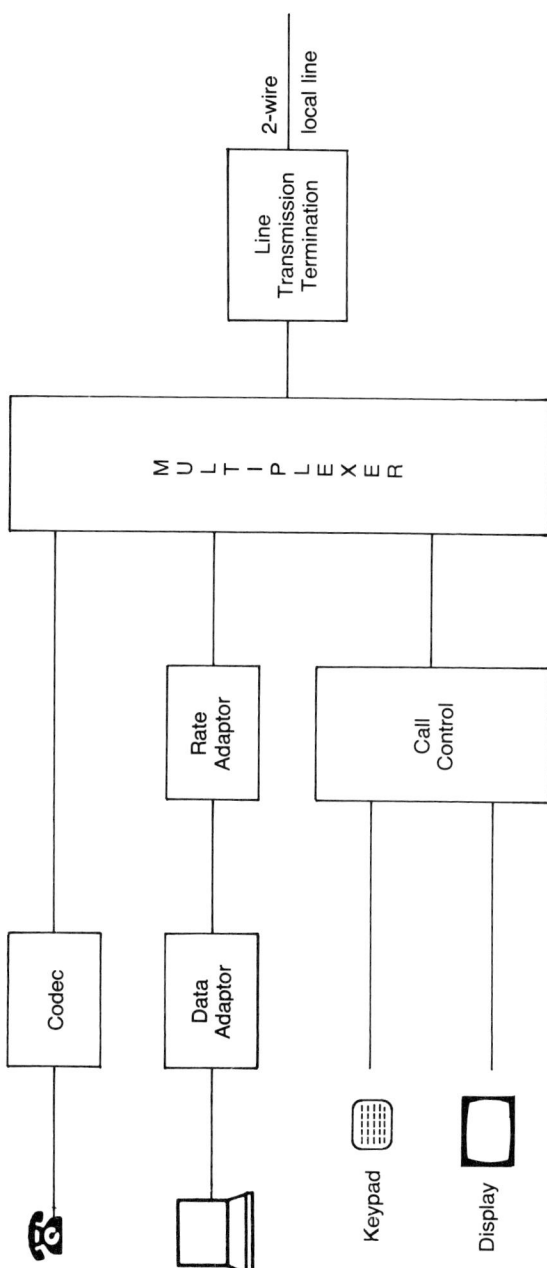

Figure 5.4 NTE Functional Diagram

The MODEC is a combined modem and codec, working at up to 300 bit/s which allows communication between low-speed RS232 terminals connected to IDA and similar terminals connected to the PSTN via modems.

The 2-wire analogue interface enables existing analogue equipment, including answering machines, modems and existing Prestel sets, to interwork between ISDN and PSTN.

The NTE is connected to the ISDN local exchange, either directly by an existing local cable pair or via a local cable pair connected to a multiplexer located remote from the exchange and connected to the exchange via a 2048 Kbit/s link (Figure 5.5). The multiplexers are provided to reduce the number of 80 Kbit/s circuits in the local networks and to serve users on the fringe of local distribution cables.

IDA Signalling

The separate IDA signalling channel (channel D) means that the System X common channel signalling feature is extended to the user. User network control messages are transferred between the NTE and ISDN exchange on IDA links using the digital access signalling system DASS. DASS is a message-based common channel signalling system in which variable length message frames are transferred over the 8 Kbit/s signalling channel for both user channels. Wherever possible the general provisions in respect of High-Level Data Link Control (HDLC) procedures, as defined by the ISO, are followed.

This type of message-based signalling system permits the exchange to send call progress information to the user for presentation. This is necessary on digital calls since no in-band announcements or tones are permitted on this type of call in order to avoid interference with data communications. The call progress information is presented to the user by means of an alphanumeric display on the NTE (1 and 3), by in-band tones, a tone-caller or via the X.21 interface to the data terminal. DASS is an interim standard developed by BT prior to the availability of an international standard for IDA signalling.

As shown in Figure 5.5, the new generation of digital PBXs can

OPTIONS FOR THE FUTURE

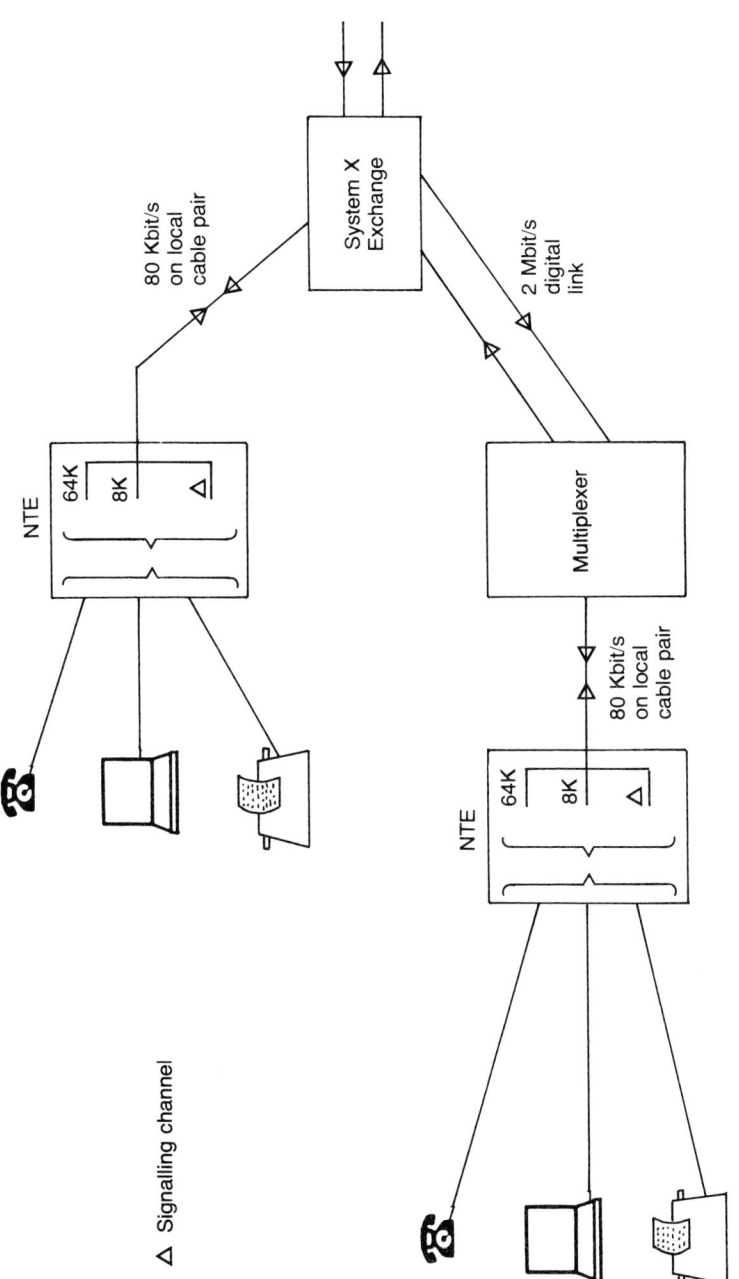

Figure 5.5   ISDN Connections

be provided with a 2048 Kbit/s (multi-line) digital link to the ISDN exchange, provided the PBX conforms to the IDA signalling protocol DASS. The PBX connects directly to the IDA line such that up to 30 simultaneous 64 Kbit/s channels are available, and provides network terminating functions and switching between the IDA line and its extensions. DASS transfers variable length message frames on the common 64 Kbit/s signalling channel of the 2 Mbit/s link for all 30 user channels.

A variety of voice and non-voice terminals can be connected as extensions supporting a number of services (Integrated Services PBX). The ISPBX extensions may be NTEs or equivalent, or the ISPBX may perform the functions normally carried out by an NTE.

IDA provides access to a number of services which utilise the opportunities of high-speed digital connections, for example:

— a new circuit switched digital data service operating at data rates of up to 48 Kbit/s;

— Digital Private Circuit Service: KiloStream SP (Semi-Permanent); functionally identical to KiloStream but provided via IDA switched connections (digital point-to-point links at 2400, 4800, 8000, 9600 bit/s, 48 and 64 Kbit/s). For some years this will not be an economically viable alternative to private circuits for most users;

— Asynchronous Data Service: a service to be provided for an interim period only to allow for existing V-series terminals operation at up to 1900 bit/s via X.21 bis interface.

The above group of IDA services are bearers that can be used to carry other services. Further IDA services are those which can be accessed more efficiently using IDA. These include:

— Packet SwitchStream (PSS);
— videotex;
— Teletex;
— telephony;
— facsimile;
— slowscan TV.

Satellite Business Networks

Satellite communications is another vehicle to integrate voice and data services. The advantages of satellite systems lie in their inherent distance-insensitivity, multiple-access capability, large geographical coverage and high data rates. With Time Division Multiple Access (TDMA) and small-size earth stations, satellite networks can achieve a high degree of resource sharing and facilitate on-demand configurability under user control.

Business Communications Systems

PABXs have undergone a similar digital evolution. Users' computer-controlled PABXs are natural vehicles to facilitate the integration of voice and data although baseband and broadband coaxial cable systems are emerging as alternative technologies.

Today, virtually all PABX manufacturers consider data capability including X.25 interface support as a basic requirement for existing and future products. Future PABXs will incorporate a much wider range of data capabilities.

Users' extensions are also targets for integration in the 1980s; product announcements today include the combination of telephone set, terminal and intelligent processor into a single extension unit.

Being of prime interest to most organisations, these types of developments in business communications are likely to have a very significant impact on the shape of corporate communications networks. Many of these aspects are considered in greater detail in Chapter 6.

6 Integrated Voice and Data in the Office

AN OVERVIEW

It is expected that business office communications requirements during the 1980s will extend beyond traditional voice and data. They will include text or document communications and image communications. Text and document communications needs are growing as a consequence of the rapidly expanding word processing market as well as through the efforts currently directed at the automation of many office functions. Image communications is likely to emerge from improvements in areas such as facsimile, graphics and video workstations as an integral part of the office automation route accelerated by a need to minimise both mail and travel costs. A further requirement for communication is also emerging from the continuing pressure to manage and control office energy costs and to monitor security and fire detection systems.

The cost of providing office communications is affected by a number of factors. These include the bandwidth or data rate requirements of the services, the number of workstations requiring access to the services, plus the level of cost sharing of common resources, such as workstation equipment, central processing and control equipment and interconnecting site communications media.

The number and use of services/workstations plus the allocation of shared resources is very much dependent upon specific user requirements.

Voice communications has been implemented over the years by transmitting voice signals in analogue form over relatively inexpensive copper wire pairs between telephone instruments via circuit switching arrangements. The bandwidth required for analogue voice is 4 KHz. However, the cables serving these connections are capable of carrying Megabit digital signals.

The introduction of digital switching principles in PABXs is now common. Currently, digitally encoded voice requires 64 Kbit/s for PCM transmission. However, lower speed voice transmission through a variety of encoding schemes is achievable and in the future more efficient coding schemes at 32 Kbit/s will be used.

Both low-speed asynchronous and high-speed synchronous data communications can be carried over this same wiring. Most user applications, however, require some type of transmission modulation system to achieve acceptable error performance over typical building/site distances.

Image communications requirements vary widely between applications. For example low-speed facsimile can be carried at speeds in the Kilobit per second range, whereas high-speed facsimile operates in the tens of Kilobits per second range. Graphic workstations can require data rates in the order of 100 Kilobits per second.

Video workstation requirements vary from the Kilobit per second range (for still pictures) to the Megabit per second range (for moving pictures). All these requirements can be handled by standard building telephone wiring.

Sensors and actuators associated with office surveillance systems generate signals in the Kilobit per second range which can also be carried on the telephone wiring.

INTEGRATION OF SERVICES

Office automation envisages service and workstation concepts which integrate all the above areas of office communications. The problem which faces the prospective user is how best to provide these services in his own office environment. Current approaches centre around the interconnection of shared resources and individual terminals and workstations via bus networks, ring networks and star networks (see Figure 6.1).

In many existing data networks, dedicated terminals are usually

INTEGRATED VOICE AND DATA IN THE OFFICE 71

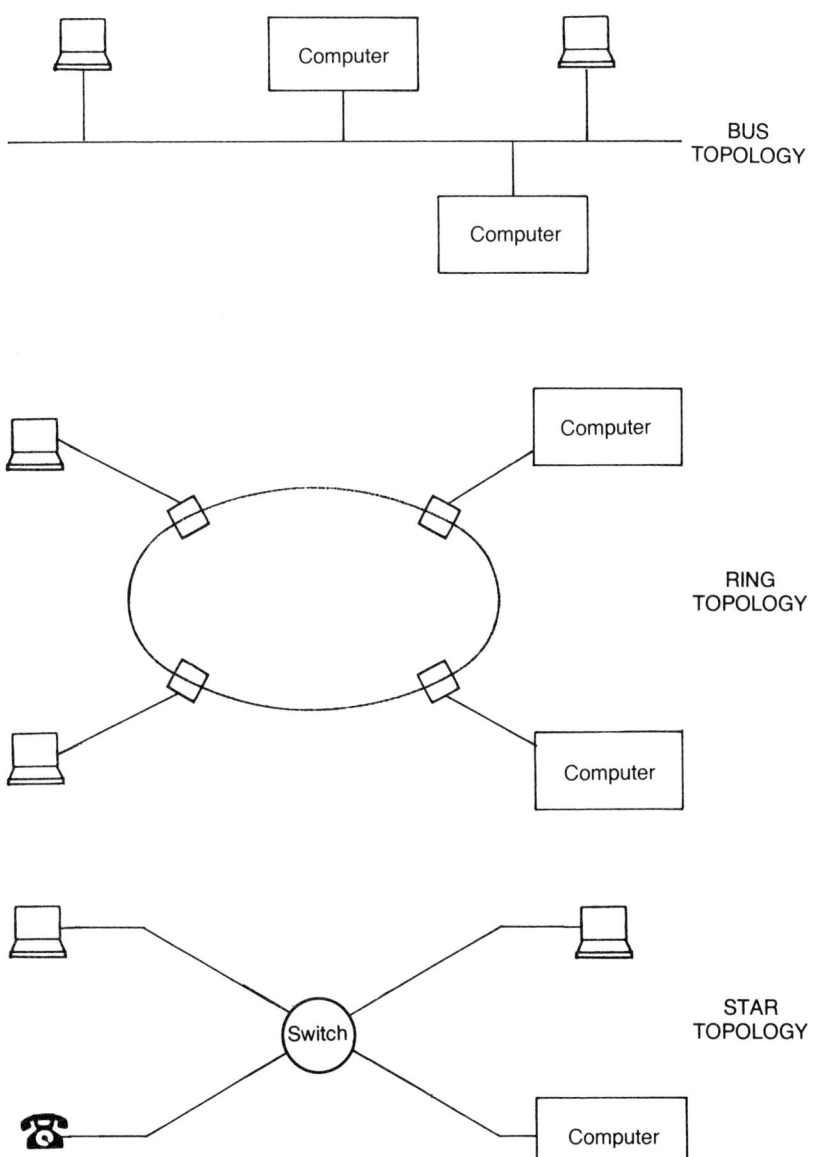

Figure 6.1 Office Communications Network Topologies

connected to a specific host computer over multi-dropped private telephone wiring. In this arrangement the host typically controls communication within the network by polling each of the terminals in turn. This is the type of approach common in bus networks.

Other types of bus networks are currently receiving considerable attention for applications involving the data communication needs of office automation systems. These usually involve a wide bandwidth medium operating at Megabits per second, such as coaxial cable, which is shared by multiple users. Different approaches have been adopted in the control of such networks such as centralised control, CSMD, etc. Other designs involve the use of token passing to give each terminal equal access opportunity to the bus.

At present no commercial bus system offers voice services. It is possible to carry packetised digital voice over such a network but limitations such as the cost of speech packetising and bandwidth compression, together with impairment in the quality of voice transmission, suggest that packetising on a bus system is not yet an optimum solution for voice communications.

Ring networks are similar to bus networks in terms of communication media used, control techniques and switching techniques.

Star networks are used in all office buildings to connect telephones to PABXs over twisted copper pairs. Virtually all buildings are wired in a pattern that interconnects workstations with centralised equipment over a number of floors interconnected by multi-pair cables between floors. Integrated office communications based on this wiring has the obvious advantage of economy because it avoids the need to install additional communications media and offers a capability of carrying Megabit per second bandwidths.

In order to provide the flexible total switching system or integrated area network that users require for business communications of the future, the PABX needs to provide a distributed switching system. Hence PABX suppliers are currently developing PABXs capable of operating in a distributed processing role.

In this form the PABX is not provided as a single central controlled installation, but as a number of smaller sub-systems installed on different floors of the same building or even different sites, inter-

INTEGRATED VOICE AND DATA IN THE OFFICE

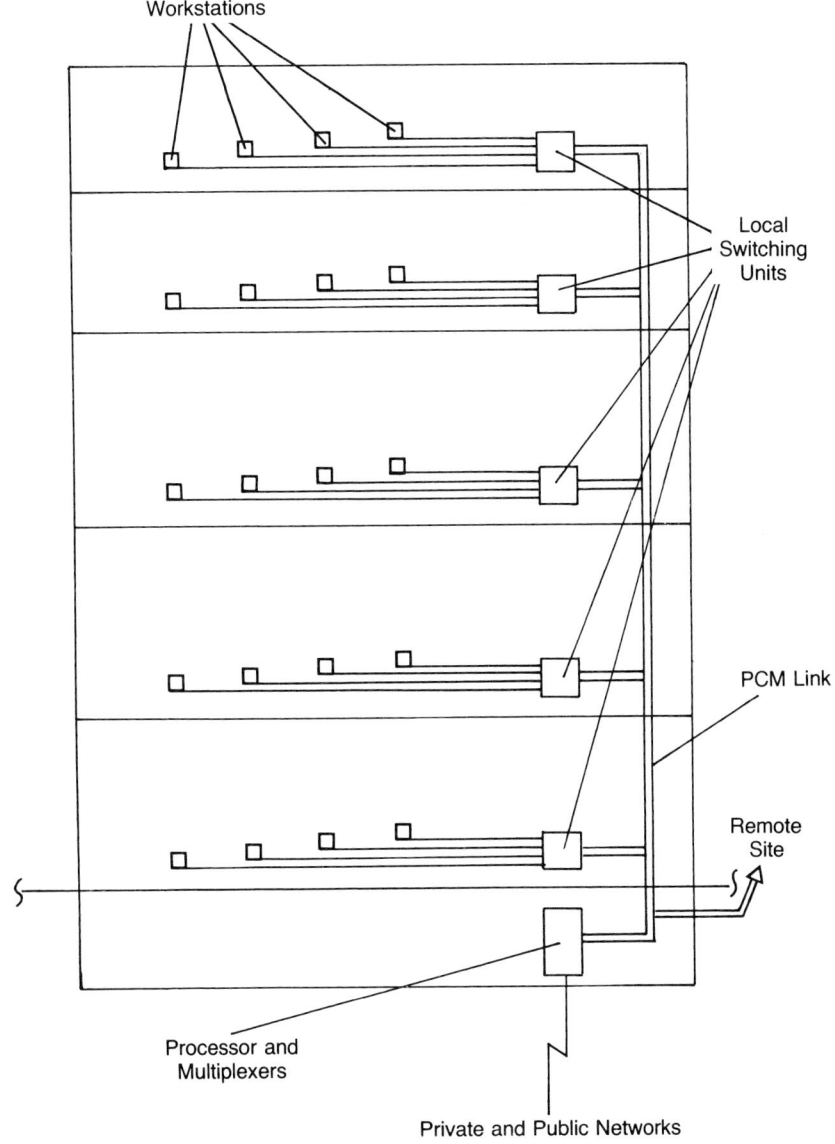

Figure 6.2 Distributed PABX

linked by PCM connections (Figure 6.2). The processing unit is connected to the various switching units via high-level multiplexers with varying transmission speeds. The PABX distributed switching system is based on the same digital hierarchies as the digital networks with the multiplexers providing for transmission speeds ranging over 2, 8, 34 and 140 Mbit/s. This enables switching units to be sited remotely and to communicate via digital networks provided by BT or Mercury.

In the example shown, the central processing unit and multiplexer unit are located together, perhaps in a basement, and connected via 2 Mbit/s links to switching units on each floor of the building with each switch connected to workstations on that floor. Such an installation minimises the amount of cabling between floors.

PABX suppliers are approaching the development of distributed systems along these lines although differing in detail in terms of the modularity of system design and the extent to which the integration of services is immediately possible.

PABX DEVELOPMENTS

In the last decade the PABX has undergone a digital evolution starting with the development of the stored program controlled (SPC) exchange which commenced with the announcement of the IBM 3750, an analogue SPC exchange, in the early-1970s. Since that time, all manufacturers in the UK have announced, and in the main installed, SPC exchanges either as their own developments or as purchases from other countries anglicised to meet BT requirements. Computer-controlled PABXs are natural vehicles to facilitate the integration of voice and data. Today virtually all PABX manufacturers consider data capability, including X.25 support, as a basic requirement for existing and future products.

A typical product installed today provides voice interfaces with public networks through central office loops, two- and four-wire E & M trunks, and direct dialling. Data transmission is facilitated by means of incoming and outgoing modem pools in which the PABX determines the characteristics of the data transmission and selects the correct modem. For packet switching applications an X.25 interface is added to connect the data equipment to both public and private packet switching systems. For compatible and proprietary terminal equipment, the switch provides a transparent connection; in the case of incompatible terminals, the switch is programmed to support protocol conversion for speed, code and transmission. Used in conjunction with any terminal device that uses standard interfaces, the PABX provides for data communications at bit rates up to 19.6 Kbit/s in asynchronous mode and 56 Kbit/s in synchronous mode.

The provision of a transparent connection from terminal to the 64 Kbit/s PABX highway permits the transmission of voice and data simultaneously between terminals and via intelligent gateways in the PABX across external public networks. With the anticipated growth in digital networks, a digital format can be maintained across both local systems and the national networks; for example, a synchronous or asynchronous data terminal can be connected through the local digital PABX (64 Kbit/s) over a PCM link to a remote PABX and switched through to another terminal with the 8-bit CCITT format retained throughout the network.

A significant advantage in exploiting the opportunities for voice/data integration is the ability of the PABX to gain access to external networks and facilities. Here the PABX acts as a gateway to shared resources, such as electronic messaging and computing facilities, and external telecommunication services, such as electronic mail systems and Teletex. Compatibility with all new services and future facilities such as Teletex, X-Stream and Mercury offers a wide range of network alternatives.

INTEGRATED NETWORK SERVICES

As we have seen earlier, telephone administrations throughout the world are planning to provide the Integrated Services Digital Network (ISDN) capable of offering voice, data and image network services. Preparation of standards for the ISDN is under way in several study groups of CCITT 7, 11 and 18.

Extension of the ISDN to users' voice and data terminals or digital PBXs, by building onto the digital switching and transmission systems already in use, is an integral part of these plans. The integrated voice and data workstation concept is an essential component in the provision of integrated office services along with the proposed generalised digital station format as the common access format.

ISDN also offers the opportunities of public network capabilities together with a variety of new services and facilities to business communication planners in addition to private network options.

As ISDN services become available it will become increasingly prudent to select an office communications system architecture well matched to ISDN to ensure minimal network interfacing costs without sacrificing network service options. PABX compatibility with System X and ISDN may be the most important capability to users in the UK: it offers a far more sophisticated public network in which numerous facilities and integrated digital voice/data links direct to the PABX are provided. The acceleration of the System X implementation plans now makes it more important for PABXs to be completely compatible with System X, IDA and ISDN.

Proprietary digital communication protocols are being incorporated in architectures of office products which are intended to be upwards compatible with the emerging ISO and CCITT standards.

The ISDN approach implies that data communications can be provided to any workstation along with voice, at any time, via a universal wall socket and normal building wiring. In this way, office information automation can grow in response to users' needs. A flexible digital format of protocols is essential to interface smoothly with emerging international standards, to provide sufficient bandwidth to workstations for the foreseeable future, and to have the capacity to grow to wider bandwidth as market needs develop.

INTEGRATION OF SERVICES IN PRIVATE NETWORKS

Traditional separate voice and data networks have been implemented by the majority of larger organisations for many reasons, including a need to ensure reliability and to avoid potential conflict for services. But in many instances such networks were created because the technology up to the early-1980s was inadequate for successful integration of voice and data.

PABXs of non-SPC design offered a maximum data transfer

rate of only 1200 bit/s and did not provide any store-and-forward facilities. This meant that acceptable response times from data terminals were not available when switching data through a PABX. Equally the ability of PABXs to provide a full network with tandem switching of both voice and data through the same system to an organisation's various locations was limited by the necessity for the services to contend for lines through the switch.

One major advantage of the new SPC technology is that the facility of 'virtual data channels' provides a guaranteed path through the system at any time for data or text communications. This enables a PABX to act as an efficient and cheap switching node for data services as well as voice.

Effective networks can therefore now be configured for the switching of data and voice through common systems. Using the delta configuration (shown in Figure 6.3) allows for the situation where, if a major trunk connection goes down between two major switching centres, data can be re-routed around the remaining network – providing high reliability. In this way the potential of the new digital services can further realise the major cost reductions achievable and at the same time can be used to improve the reliability of networks.

The major advantage of such a network is that facilities such as alternative routeing, route optimisation, transparency to users (different locations but common numbering and common facilities), PABX facilities (eg call-booking, follow-me), centralised network management, and cost-effective voice and data integration, normally available only on single PABXs, can now be extended throughout the entire network, irrespective of the type of traffic. However, to provide effective networking there is a need for network management control functions which have the ability to monitor the network to determine the status of *all* services at any time and to re-allocate channels dynamically to ensure effective switching of all services contending for use of the network. For example, if a need for priority for data arises then voice channels may need to be re-allocated on a temporary basis.

Such management facilities are not yet available from traditional PABX suppliers but are being developed. Within a reasonably short timescale it is likely that effective management control

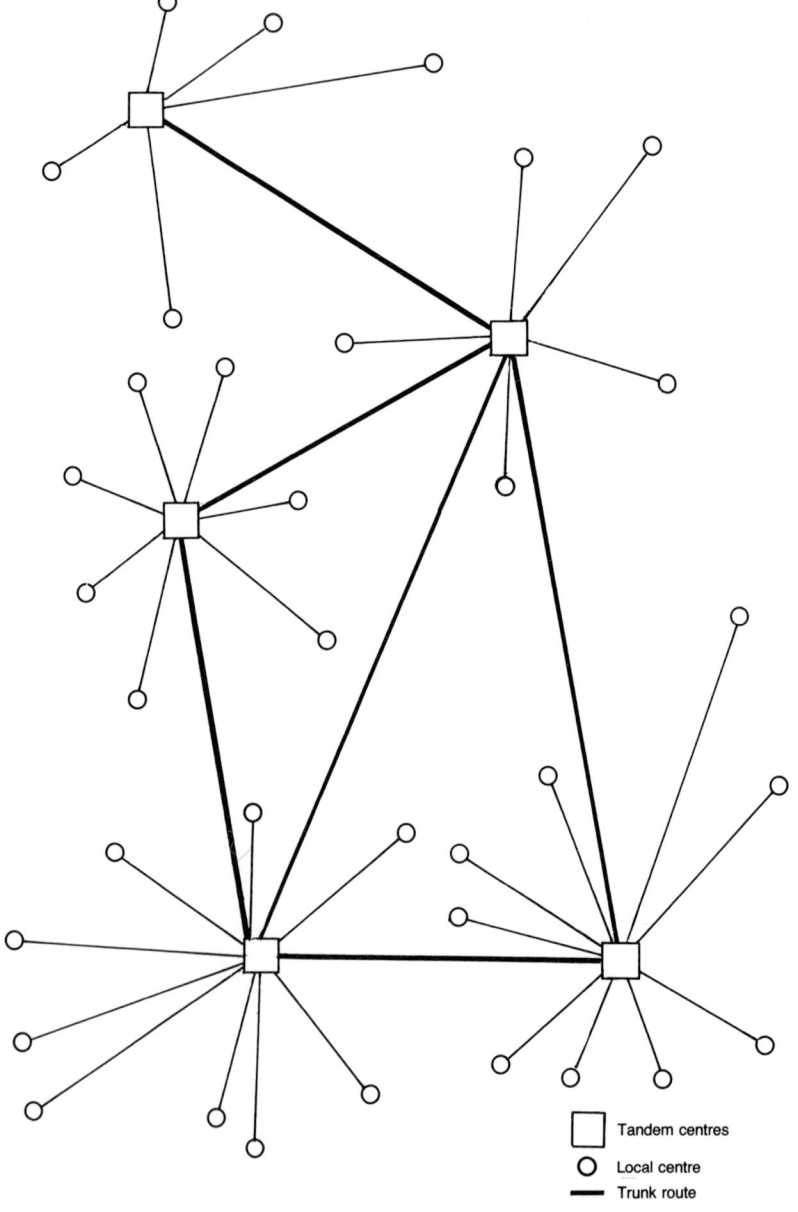

Figure 6.3   Use of Tandem Centres in Large Networks

will be made available for comprehensive management of integrated services. Meanwhile the move towards integrated services is possible using the best combination of management facilities currently available with the separate services.

7 Network Strategy for the Eighties

INTRODUCTION

Information Technology embraces all forms of information within an organisation; for example, voice, data, text, image, fax and video. It is now recognised that information should be regarded as a corporate resource. This fact, together with a need to make vital business decisions rapidly, creates an overriding corporate need for effective *business communications*. Business communications is therefore very much a part of the Information Technology of the organisation and as such is a concern for data processing (DP), office automation (OA), and telecommunications.

Today communications should be seen as *an opportunity*. An organisation which gets its business communications strategy right will find that it can do a great deal more with its DP and OA.

WHY A STRATEGY?

Most large organisations currently employ separate dedicated communications networks for telephony, data traffic and telex. Within data processing itself, it is not uncommon to find several independent networks dedicated to specific applications. With the inevitable proliferation of computers, data and text terminals around the office over the next five to ten years, this dedicated approach will seriously constrain and limit the effectiveness of each type of communications. We should note:

— the inefficiencies inherent in the use of dedicated facilities; for example, separate voice and data terminals on a manager's desk;

- the problems resulting from the sharing of data files between separate applications;
- confusion over interface standards.

THE BENEFITS OF A STRATEGY

In addition to avoiding problems inherent in the dedicated approach, the development of a corporate communications strategy will also benefit communications management in three important ways:

- *by facilitating a planned response to technological and market uncertainties.* With the multitude of communications products and services being developed and anticipated over the next five years (following 'liberalisation', and 'privatisation' of services, and technological change), management need a clear picture of their objectives in order to make the correct purchase decisions. A long-term plan is the essential basis for prudent product and service purchasing policies;
- *by ensuring a timely response to changing user needs.* To anticipate future user need, for both existing and new communications services, strategic planners need to take into account changes in business plans (eg growth/reduction, site closures/expansion, increased use of office automation, adoption of video conferencing). Therefore an increasing need for a continuing dialogue between business and communications planners and between planners and users will develop;
- *by securing support from top management.* The very scope and nature of an organisation-wide corporate communications strategy must carry the support of top management if it is to be successfully implemented. In particular, because it will inevitably involve the organisation in large capital outlays, close and regular contact with top management will be necessary to enable planners to gain support for investments which may not be immediately justifiable on cost savings alone. An understanding at the top of the long-term benefits will help to secure management commitment to the total strategy.

ORGANISATIONAL ISSUES

Many of the organisations interviewed are still organised to manage the different types of communications in separate parts of the organisational structure. For example, it is quite usual to find the following activities managed and controlled by different departments:

— data processing (and hence data communications);

— telephones and telex;

— office systems (and hence inter word processor communications);

— radio communications;

— scientific and engineering communications (eg process control and telemetry).

Each of these separate telecommunications responsibilities is also typically characterised by acting autonomously in the provisioning of equipment and services and by interacting with other telecommunications functions only occasionally and usually only at crisis time. In this situation the following organisational deficiencies are likely to occur:

— little or no co-ordination of network development;

— multiple interface points with BT;

— unco-ordinated budgets leading to over-expenditure;

— unco-ordinated standards (resulting in unnecessary expenditure, lock-in situations, barriers to open systems and integration, etc);

— no long-term strategic goals and plans.

This type of fragmented management structure which may only converge, if at all, at a very senior level of management (for example, at Board level) is totally inappropriate for the planning of corporate communications networks.

A realisation of the fact that a communications network is a corporate resource to be managed like any other organisational resource, paves the way for the integration of services and the planning of systems from a corporate viewpoint. It is therefore not surprising to see in larger organisations the emergence of Information Systems Departments created to ensure that plans for DP, OA and communications are developed in harmony.

ORGANISING FOR INFORMATION TECHNOLOGY (IT)

An approach to developing an 'Information Systems' organisation which will match the corporate strategies and structure of an organisation typically involves four steps:

— identification of the role of IT within the organisation;

— identification of the level and type of information transferred between users of IT;

— development of a corporate IT strategy;

— establishment of an IT organisation to implement the corporate strategy.

The significance and function of IT in business units are largely determined by the nature of the business. For example, in businesses such as retail banking and insurance, the role of IT is today becoming a dominant factor and has a significant impact on the business strategy adopted. In airline reservation and mail order organisations the implementation of the business strategy is very much dependent upon IT. In other industries, particularly those in the retailing and manufacturing sectors, IT is needed but does not appear to be as crucial in providing a major competitive advantage.

In all organisations the function of IT is very closely related to the nature of information communicated both internally and externally. It is therefore necessary to establish the level and type of information transferred internally (at least between departments) and externally between business units, between departments and external sources (such as customers, suppliers, agents, dealers, etc) and between business units and head office. The amount of information and type of information transferred between business units and from business units to head office is variable and often difficult to determine: it is dependent upon a number of factors, such as the level of inter-trading, the nature of the corporate administration (eg reporting levels) and the rate of introduction of office technology. Consideration of the role of IT and identification of information transfers show that for different businesses, quite different IT strategies are likely to emerge.

DEVELOPING A CORPORATE IT STRATEGY

Information Technology embraces all forms of information within an organisation. Therefore it is important that every organisation, whatever its size, should develop IT strategies to address business needs and thus be in a position to make maximum use of technological developments as they become appropriate. Planning at this level involves many strategic issues; in particular, business planning, major systems requirements planning and definition of the technical shape of information processing. It is also necessary to formulate technical strategies for office automation, data processing and communications networks. Apart from the formulation of a strategy for corporate communications networks – later treated as the major subject – these high-level planning activities are beyond the scope of this book. Therefore, in the ensuing discussions leading to the development of a strategy for communications it will be assumed that all these other levels of planning have been completed. In many organisations this will not be so and, consequently, some guidance from Board level on the flexibility required in the design of the network in relation to business plans will be required; for example, to allow for expansion in the business, and to provide for the possibility of take-overs or 'disinvestment'.

RESOLVE STRATEGIC ISSUES FIRST

In all cases senior management must be involved in establishing the strategic telecommunications plan for the organisation. Examples of strategic plan elements which need establishing at this level include:

— the prime end uses for the network(s) and other telecommunications resources which may be acquired;

— the degree of integration desired for data, voice, text and image information (office and messaging systems);

— the basic architecture of the data network; for example,

mainframe host or multiple minicomputer hosts;
— the organisational groups which must participate in the feasibility and planning studies;
— other design concepts required for telecommunications, such as the extent to which Value Added Networks or PSS should be considered instead of leased-line facilities;
— the organisational structure and staffing needed at the feasibility and planning stages.

This last element is particularly challenging due to the competing areas of interests within organisations. For example, *data processing* staff are usually involved with data communications and often see their role enlarging to embrace telecommunications; *office management* staff see their function including office automation. Both run headlong into *administration* where traditional voice and messaging services such as telex and facsimile are handled.

The introduction of local networks for the integration of electronic office equipment and the combined use of voice, data and text services adds a new element which is difficult for these existing groups to grasp fully. Because re-organising presents a number of difficulties along these lines due to the widely different interests within most organisations, it is important first to set up a Corporate Telecommunications Planning group to look at all aspects of the integration question.

In adopting this approach, the organisation should:
— define the organisation required to conduct the study. In all cases it is essential to ensure that such a body reports to a high level to gain sufficient backing to advance the results of the study. It is also important to see that this body is staffed by all persons currently responsible for all the various organisational aspects associated with integration of services, at the same time recognising that it may be necessary to appoint outside specialists or consultants;
— conduct a survey of existing equipment to identify current usage and volumes of traffic and to determine new

requirements. There is a particular need here to ascertain the justification of specific applications and to determine which aspects are to be included;

— establish a 'requirements plan' which defines a detailed set of objectives which clearly state the place of integration within the overall corporate plan of the organisation. Overall a three-to-five-year planning cycle is required but the plan should also identify which short-term aspects need to be considered;

— draw up an operational control structure necessary to implement the objectives of the requirements plan which relates to the existing structure of the company or business;

— present to the 'Board' or 'controlling body' recommendations which include the identification of the operational control structure required and set out its objectives;

— obtain Board approval of the recommendations. Board involvement ensures that recommendations fit within the overall business plan.

The work of the planning group should be carefully monitored and controlled by a senior management committee. Each element in the requirements plan should be tested carefully through a cost/benefit analysis and the study group given regular directions on the resulting desired options.

Care should be taken to avoid going into detailed design work at this stage as a conceptual design is usually sufficient. Major considerations by study group members will include an on-going determination of the appropriate level of detail and the degree of integration with the organisation's overall business plan.

The group will need access to business plans, profit projections, market forecasts, projected re-organisations and so forth. Executive approval of the direction in which the planning group is moving will greatly assist the access to this basic planning data.

The strategic issues review should lead to a clear and positive senior management commitment. If it does not, then the organisation faces a severely reduced telecommunications potential. If this is the case, then this must be reflected by the scaling down of planned end uses, and the scope and level of integration anticipated in the organisation's telecommunications resources.

DESIGN THE OPERATIONAL MANAGEMENT GROUP

Having developed a corporate strategy for Information Technology, and resolved at top level the strategic issues relating to the establishment of the telecommunications plan, it is now possible to design a corporate operations group to execute this strategy based upon the recommendations of the planning group. Such recommendations will have identified the form of operational control required and set out its objectives according to the particular organisational requirements over the short term and longer three-to-five-year timescale. What now remains is a decision on the degree of centralisation and control to be sought within the IT group.

Control of overall strategy can range from the complete autonomy of business units, through central guidance and co-ordination, in which consultancy and corporate-wide facilities are provided, to a totally integrated/centralised strategy, in which the corporate group dominates policies and the implementation of facilities.

Similar degrees of control and centralisation can be applied to:

— financial and budgetary procedures;

— the level of standardisation, eg from nil to total;

— corporate facilities in terms of networks, computing resources, etc;

— responsibilities of corporate staff, eg from advisory only, through guidance and co-ordination of specifications and operations, to absolute control of decisions and operations;

— criteria for investment, eg from local, corporate evaluation techniques, to corporate standards.

For each area of IT (ie data processing, office automation and telecommunications) a strategy will be selected which matches the degree of centralisation and control required. In telecommunications this could vary from complete freedom from centralisation, through the establishment of central guidelines for external interfaces and telecommunications links, to the complete co-ordination of both voice and data services in the form of corporate wide area and local area networks. The most extreme degree of control might include a fully integrated and centralised policy with centralised financial and budgetary procedures and employing integrated voice/data/text/and image networks.

A more autonomous strategy might be suitable within the organisation in which the role of IT differs considerably between business units and where there is little interaction between units; for example, the organisation with a number of subsidiaries manufacturing proprietary goods at dispersed sites with only a minimum of communication with head office. In this situation it is probable that the strategy will revolve around centralised group guidance but with autonomy retained locally by the subsidiaries. On the other hand, an organisation in which the business units are more integrated functionally requires the adoption of an integrated strategy. In practice, it is likely that a mixed strategy will evolve.

The final planning stage involves planning related to people ('people planning'). It is on this aspect of planning that the telecommunications strategy will succeed or flounder. An organisation cannot expect to implement and manage a highly complex telecommunications network without the appropriate levels of planning, management, operations and support skills. Therefore the planning stage must include the planning of people to implement, operate, maintain and manage the telecommunications service.

Clearly the operational group must fit the kind of strategy adopted in defining the overall IT strategy. With integrated/centralised strategies the normal form adopted would be a strong central group of people with total operational responsibility. With autonomous strategies the central organisation becomes less of a requirement but practically it might be sensible to locate specialists at a central function with consultant or advisory roles.

Within the group it may be necessary to split the operations function from the planning and design function to ensure that service criteria are constantly met. Overall, data processing, office automation, and communications functions need to respond to a single function at a senior level within the organisation. With an autonomous strategy it may be more appropriate to split the network planning and operation functions away from the consultancy function because of the increased need for the servicing of the business units' requirements in the consultancy area.

Within the telecommunications function, the move towards the integration of services makes it necessary to address certain organisational aspects in order to make such a strategy achievable and effective; in particular, the reporting responsibility for different forms of communications. It is also important to pull together the appropriate mix of skills, required to cover the traditional areas of data communications and voice communications, together with a good understanding of all the other forms of communications. A combination of voice, data, carrier, private industry, and of appropriate international knowledge and expertise is necessary under the sole direction of a single person charged with overall responsibility for the management of both voice and data networks.

8 Elements of a Communications Strategy

INTRODUCTION

Having established the degree of centralisation relevant to the strategy to be adopted, and having designed the organisation to fit the overall requirements, it is now possible to develop the strategic plan in depth and lay definitive milestones for the implementation of the corporate network.

A strategy can never be a complete statement of fact because of the uncertainty of future developments and events. It can however act as a signpost pointing the direction towards a recommended goal or end-point some time in the future.

The first element in a communications strategy is therefore a definition of the goal.

DEFINING THE GOAL

Within a timescale of five to ten years, the goal of any strategy can today only be seen as a loose series of guidelines upon which a more specific plan can evolve as developments within the industry crystalise. The concept of an open integrated network which brings together all types of information and a multitude of applications is still not clearly defined by the industry or the standards bodies. However, discussions with UK private and public organisations and the general consensus of informed opinion signify that, given the inevitability of increased use of information technology and the projected developments in the technology described earlier, the majority of large organisations will adopt an open integrated network as the basis of their corporate business communications

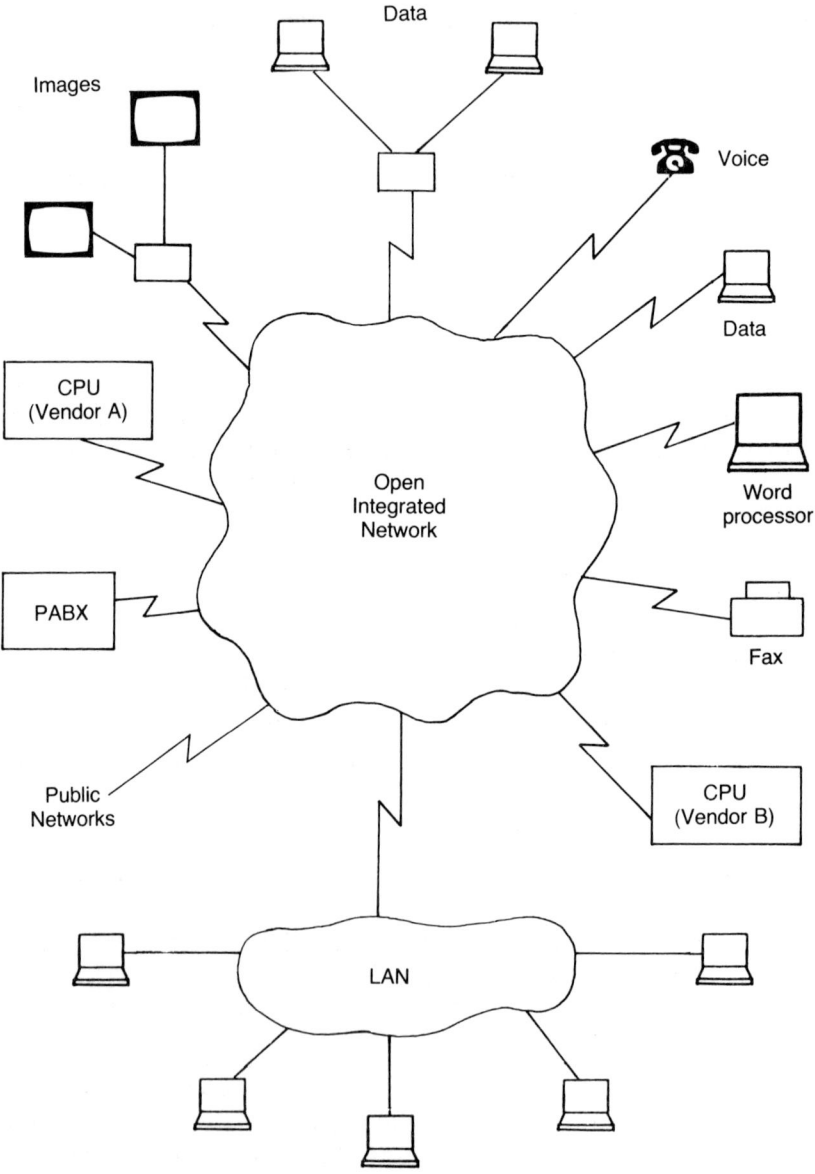

Figure 8.1 Open Integrated Network

ELEMENTS OF A COMMUNICATIONS STRATEGY

strategy goal over the next decade. An *open integrated network* can provide the facilities to:

— attach all types of terminals; for example, telephones, data, fax, images, etc;
— support any computer applications regardless of supplier;
— interconnect all devices attached to the network;
— enable interworking between all devices.

Such a network (Figure 8.1) establishes a specific framework which defines how the various components fit together. These are likely to include terminals, terminal controllers and processors, switching equipment and communications links. The way in which each component communicates with each of the other components is governed by the rules established within the network architecture.

STANDARDS IN IT

Standards are very important within this framework because it is essentially a distributed technology dependent for its effectiveness on communications. It is also a multi-vendor technology with components being provided by different suppliers.

At present, interlinking and interworking standards tend to be set by manufacturers to cover their own products. This obviously creates a problem if open networking is envisaged.

Standards which provide data communications and system interworking and which are fundamental to the IT concept are being developed within the framework of Open Systems Interconnection (OSI). OSI standards are designed to allow the exchange of information between computer systems and terminals regardless of make or geographical location.

Communications in information systems can be considered as comprising two parts; interconnection and interworking. Interconnection is the transport of information from the output of a source device to the input of a destination device; interworking is the mutually intelligible dialogue which takes place between the two connected devices. The OSI standards cover both interconnection and interworking but are independent of the actual applications; for example, word processing, database access, financial processing, etc, which are subject to other specialised standards.

OSI standards have been under development in the International Standards Organisation (ISO) since 1977. A requirement for interlinking and interworking standards has led to the development of the Basic Reference Model for OSI as a framework for the standards.

The OSI Reference Model defines the functions of each standard and the relationship between each standard, and is the accepted framework for the many organisations contributing to the OSI standardisation programme, including ISO, CCITT, ECMA, and IEEE committees. The model structures the protocols, necessary to support interworking, into seven independent functional layers: physical, data link, network, transport, session, presentation, and application. The functions provided by one layer are used by the layer above to provide enhanced facilities.

INTERCEPT STRATEGY

The process of international standardisation takes a long time. To speed up the introduction into the UK of the OSI international standards the government has drawn up a list of Intercept Recommendations which cover OSI services and protocols.

In some cases these recommendations are anticipations of the outcome of work on OSI by the ISO; in others, they are restatements of previously ambiguous or multi-choice standards; and, in yet other cases, they indicate the best way forward where currently available standards are most likely to be replaced. The criteria for making Intercept Recommendations are:

— widespread agreement on the function of, and need for, the standard;

— a high degree of international technical agreement;

— a credible source;

— an assured future.

The confidence level behind intercepts is such that they should all mature into full standards. They should never be withdrawn or fulfil only temporary functions.

For some time it will not be possible to intercept all the desired standards, as international work in many areas is not sufficiently stable. This means that some layers of the ISO seven-layer reference model will not be covered by Intercept. To overcome this problem a number of 'interim recommendations' will be made.

The first recommendations were announced in February 1983, with source documents and supplementary technical guides covering all the recommendations in the first intercept list being made available by the end of the year. New recommendations will be added whenever the necessary criteria are satisfied and ultimately the intercepts will be replaced by full international standards.

In support of the recommendations there will be the documentation referred to above, tutorial materials and seminars and development aids, test facilities, reference implementations, etc. One of the support measures is the establishment of test centres. The National Computing Centre is mounting the first pilot testing scheme which is due to become operational later this year.

THE INTEGRATION QUESTION

For many organisations, particularly the multinational companies with numerous operating sites and those who are big users of information (such as the financial institutions), there is a growing demand to implement the full integration of all information services at the point of need – ie at the office desk.

It is now accepted that the concept of a fully integrated information communications service in which voice, data, text and perhaps video and facsimile traffic is transmitted simultaneously is unlikely under a two-to-five year timescale. Nevertheless, during the late-1980s, integrated communications networks will become much more prevalent in both the private corporate domain and the public service domain. Today the problem is to establish just how far this integration can be achieved.

Data Services

The integration of data services is now an accepted principle through the adoption of the OSI layered approach. This has been stimulated by a universal trend away from centralised to distributed data processing coupled with a need to have common access and equipment availability.

Voice/Data Services

The integration of voice and data is possible in the medium-term timescale (say, two to three years), with the continuing availability of cost-effective bandwidth from BT and Mercury (point-to-point links now and switched connections through ISDN/IDA in 1984/85) and the facilities of digital exchanges. An important consideration here is the question of equating the benefits of these enhanced facilities and integration opportunities against costs.

Text Services

The possibility of the integration of text into an integrated communications service is now emerging in terms of electronic mail and messaging services through developments in public services, eg telex, Teletex, PSS, and facilities provided by message switches and PABXs on private networks. However, although the technology, including the provision of gateways (for example, between telex/IPSS/PSTN) exists today, the acceptance of text by end users in terms of familiarity, friendliness and status places the full integration of text with voice and data on the much longer timescale of five years and beyond.

Image Services

The integration of image information with voice, text and data services is only likely to be feasible on a longer-term timescale, say five to ten years, because of the unknown cost of image visibility (ie colour, drawing features, etc), lack of standards for facsimile and viewdata, and the requirement for mixed-mode working (ie fax interworking with Teletex).

Evolution of Integrated Services

However, organisations need to specify systems that will be operational in the changed business environment of the late-1980s and that have the capacity to provide integrated services in the near future, as well as fulfilling their business needs of today. A popular solution lies with the new generations of digital PABXs which, in the short-to-medium term, provide a focal point for data and voice integration.

Telecommunications systems, like any other information service, should always serve the needs of the user. The communications manager has the task of assessing current and future needs and then deciding the communications services required today and in the future. This is a difficult task in any situation but particularly now, and in the foreseeable future, with the plethora of carrier services and product options emerging in the wake of liberalisation.

However, a close look at the range of services available shows that there is very little difference between the conventional services such as voice, data (using existing analogue networks) and telex, and the newer services which include the digital network and available services. In particular, ISDN provides for both conventional and new services by offering voice, data, text (including Teletex and electronic mail services), facsimile, and video communication services. In these circumstances there is a basic requirement for a system which will handle the communications needs of today based on traditional services, yet which will at the same time allow an organisation to add on whichever potentially attractive new services become of use when they are required.

Currently PABXs are used to meet conventional voice requirements and in many organisations users find this service adequate for their immediate and short-term future needs. As newer services become more widely available and cost-effective to the smaller organisations, many will wish to enhance their existing systems to include both conventional services and some of the newer services, eg Teletex and electronic mail. Again, as the ISDN and in particular the IDA service from BT develops, the demand for new services will increase. The provision of private networks which can accommodate these changes is obviously of concern to all planners of business systems. Thus it is essential that systems installed today can evolve into the full provision and integration of all new services.

The first phase in this evolution towards the integration of services is the 'add-on' stage in which black boxes such as signalling convertors, modems and multiplexers are added to an analogue or digital PABX. Add-on systems will meet the business communications needs of many organisations for several years ahead. However, to achieve true voice and data integration it is necessary to develop new switching systems. The ideal new switch should at least be:

— digital;
— totally transparent to all communications services;
— totally transparent to all communications protocols;
— compatible with all traditional telephone services' terminal equipment;
— capable of full intelligent interworking with other suppliers' systems;
— capable of implementing internationally and nationally agreed standards;
— equipped with full user message (voice and text) control facilities, such as voice store-and-forward.

The ideal switch which meets these requirements is not yet fully available, but the current generation of PABX developments is well on the route to achieving it, as well as providing the telephone and data services of today. These new PABXs are able to provide a degree of integration between voice and data. Such devices typically provide:

— digital switching architecture;
— analogue/digital conversion based on the CCITT recommendations for European PCM systems;
— digital interfaces to 2048 Kbit/s and 64 Kbit/s digital transmission links;
— integrated voice and data up to 64 Kbit/s.

Major developments forthcoming in 1983/84 are the introduction of switches working in a fully digital environment that will be

ELEMENTS OF A COMMUNICATIONS STRATEGY 99

non-blocking, provide protocol and speed conversion, and multi-function workstations which digitise speech (voice digitising codec). But above all, to provide the flexible total switching system or integrated area network that users will require, suppliers are currently endeavouring to develop PABXs capable of operating in a 'distributed processing' form. Features of this approach, described earlier, include the distribution of processor-based utilities and data processing at nodes throughout the network and the availability of operator service concentration at a single site within the network.

The ISDN Connection

Public ISDN is based on BT service using 80 Kbit/s access methods (as described in Chapter 5). Users with suitable digital PABXs can be connected directly to the ISDN exchange via a 2048 Kbit/s digital link. The suitability will be determined by:

— the type of digital encoding process used internally by the PABX;

— the ability of the PABX to directly terminate 2048 Kbit/s PCM systems without the need to use costly PCM multiplexers;

— the ability of the PABX to synchronise with the ISDN exchange;

— the ability of the PABX to support DASS, the digital access signalling system being specified by BT.

Current developments are aimed at meeting these requirements in face of increasing market demands. However, there are a number of issues which remain to be addressed before the full benefits of ISDN become a reality to users. These include:

— the rate of deployment of System X exchanges to form IDN and subsequently ISDN;

— the level and cost of performance provided by ISDN for data users;

— whether the cost of the basic telephony service is increased with the introduction of ISDN;

— the rate of take-up to provide maximum connectivity for all users;

— whether small PABX suppliers adopt BT standards for ISDN access;

— whether it will be more cost-effective and quicker for large users to migrate to private ISDN networks.

Overall the extent to which users will make use of any new facilities such as ISDN will remain dependent upon the prices charged and the services offered. Currently the predominant area of high cost is still the local access facility although it is expected that IDA will make considerable reductions here which will be reflected in the overall charges for the service.

As BT introduces public data services in the UK (as may also Mercury) users will be able to choose between public and private facilities.

Private ISDN Networks

For the larger private networks within the UK, the components exist to provide corporate integrated digitally-switched networks which can evolve to form the basis of a private ISDN. However, some digital PABX systems still do not have the basic capability of total digital networking because of the lack of a 2 Mbit/s digital interface, interprocessor digital signalling using a common channel signalling system (for example, CCITT Number 7 or Digital Private Network Signalling System, DPNSS), or the capability for network synchronisation. Although it is likely that this capability will be provided on most PABXs by the end of 1984, the widespread availability of integrated services business communications systems providing a complete digital 64 Kbit/s terminal to exchange connection is likely to take up to three to five years.

Local Area Networks

Speculation about the role of Local Area Networks (LANs) in this new environment continues to be promulgated by the large variety of product offerings existing in the market.

The most rational approach which is gaining support today, is to use the PABX as the general-purpose 'office controller' and to link it to one or more LANs which are primarily provided to serve functional groups with intensive computer-usage needs.

However (as seen in Chapter 6), the current developments in PABXs begin to take on the shape of LANs. On the other hand, voice compression techniques combined with the packet/variable bit rate nature of the LAN give great flexibility. The balance of service which will be given by the LAN as compared to the PABX has yet to be determined. For the time being, both the LAN and PABX would appear to have a role in most organisations.

The expected co-existence of PABXs and LANs will require either the use of a growing range of 'gateways' and protocol conversion facilities or the adoption of OSI standards by the manufacturers. In the absence of the latter, gateways will link different types of LANs either directly or via PABXs, and link LANs to wide area network facilities. Experience of this function through the Project Universe will considerably assist developments within the UK. This project – a collaborative venture between government, university research establishments, and the telecommunications industry – aims to investigate the facilities which must be developed to allow business communications over a concatenation of LANs using terrestrial and satellite networks. Particular emphasis is placed on the use of Cambridge Rings for local distribution inside single establishments.

PLANNING TO MEET THE GOAL

Although the fully integrated open network is an attractive endpoint for most large users, there are obstacles which make the achievement of such a goal unlikely in less than five to ten years.

Hindrances which have been identified today include:

— the lack of universal standards beyond level four of the ISO Model;
— problems implicit in full voice and data network integration such as:
    — limited availability of digital services in many areas of the UK;

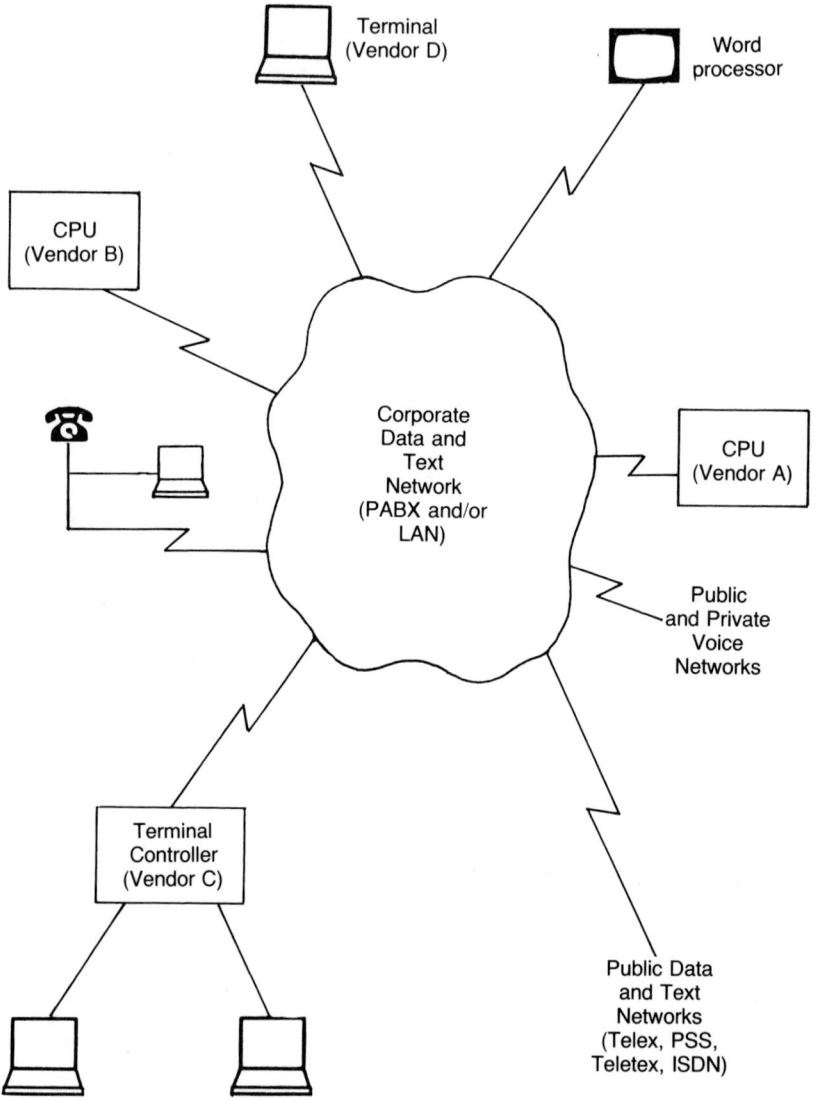

Figure 8.2 A Five-Year Goal

ELEMENTS OF A COMMUNICATIONS STRATEGY 103

— lack of availability of X.21 attachments; for example, synchronous terminals with X.21 digital interface;
— lack of low-cost high-quality voice digitising equipment;
— lack of low-cost digital single channel multiplexers;
— organisational problems such as the responsibility question, potential conflict from different demands over the same circuits, security considerations and user resistance to new technology.

In such circumstances an evolutionary approach should be adopted with limited intermediate goals. At each step the acceptable levels of network integration and the degree of 'openness' to be achieved within the network should be defined. A likely goal is illustrated by the network shown in Figure 8.2 in which support is provided for:

— terminals from several, but not an unlimited number of, suppliers;
— host computers from several, but not an unlimited number of, suppliers;
— both data and text communications;
— interface to public data network (delivery of text and data only);
— a degree of voice and data integration.

Having defined realistic goals for the five-to-ten-year period, a plan can now be evolved to formulate the strategy for the present and immediate future. Such a strategy is outlined in Chapter 9.

9 A Strategic Plan

INTRODUCTION

Different business needs require different strategies. In particular a strategy is likely to be influenced by four significant factors:

— the type of industry;

— the profitability of the organisation;

— the attitude of the organisation to technological change;

— the geographical location and size of corporate sites, ie offices, manufacturing plants, research and development centres, etc.

The strategy which follows, therefore, will not be relevant to all organisations but is based on discussions with many of the UK's larger companies. The experience gained by these organisations shows that all companies should be planning to develop their own equivalent strategies.

THE ORGANISATION

Consider the example of a large organisation with an existing private telephone network, a private message switching network and a number of data networks which have developed over the years to meet traditional data processing and scientific/technical computing requirements. In addition to voice and data communications, provision is also likely for facsimile transmission (possibly over the public network) and limited communicating word processor links.

THE OBJECTIVES

The overall objective is to plan, design and implement a corporate network end-to-end within the UK and Europe initially, and eventually worldwide, dependent upon the development of worldwide standards and their adoption by PTTs and other carriers. Such an approach will be based on the adoption of the ISO OSI standards and the interpretation of X.25 to suit needs.

A communications strategy is to be developed as an integral component of the overall IT strategy to create a strategy infrastructure which will withstand the test of time, particularly in view of new technology developments. Overall the objective is to co-ordinate telecommunications, information technology, and computing into an infrastructure of integrated services which allow user access (desk-based) to corporate information databases, electronic transfer of information worldwide, and single device access to both voice and data services.

Such a corporate strategy, which is cost-effective and meets the business needs of the organisation, must be developed. Acknowledging the very high cost of building a corporate network, such an approach is evolutionary, with limited intermediate goals and with business-related justifications for each step supported by top management.

Flexibility within the network is a prerequisite in terms of open systems interconnection and removal of all boundaries to create a general-purpose communications medium which is independent of all business systems. Efficiency is also a prerequisite in terms of the integration of services to avoid the duplication of resources such as long-haul connections and switching centres.

THE OVERALL STRATEGY

Migrate to Open Systems Interconnection

In reality, such a strategy may never be fully realised if full OSI protocol software is not made available. In such areas it is likely that low-cost microprocessors will form the basis of emulation and translation devices.

Such a strategy will need to make allowance for the adoption of the DoI intercept strategy on the course of standards for OSI. In this context there will be three levels of standards available in the UK:

— full BSI/ISO/CCITT standards;

— Intercept Recommendations;

— Interim Recommendations.

To date, the OSI Reference Model has reached international standard status and many suppliers are now offering their support for the ISO model.

There is some stability in the levels of the model but as yet these have not achieved standard status. For instance, ISO currently has two documents at Draft Proposal status for the Transport layer (DP8072 Transport Service; DP8073 Transport Protocol).

Until international standards are agreed and in use, network facilities are only available to users of terminals or applications programs provided by the suppliers of the network, or of machines which successfully emulate them. This is the concept of proprietary 'lock-in' as it generates a strong influence to acquire compatible-only equipment, simply to allow existing investments to be fully exploited. Such a concept must be fully recognised in establishing a strategy for open systems interconnection. In practice this could result in a two-stage approach towards the gradual adoption of OSI interworking protocols in place of proprietary ones. For example, stage one, which could last from say 1983 to 1986, would still exploit proprietary protocols from proprietary machine A to non-proprietary machines B and C (see Figure 9.1) but at the same time gradually introduce OSI protocols between non-proprietary machines B and C. Stage two, from 1986 onwards would gradually replace all proprietary communications protocols with their OSI equivalents. Such an approach would enable existing investments to be fully exploited and at the same time allow the gradual adoption of OSI protocols thereby providing a smooth introduction of new communications techniques and opening up the way to bring in equipment from other suppliers much more easily.

The commitment to open systems interconnection is a very positive and real thing when faced with the establishment of a

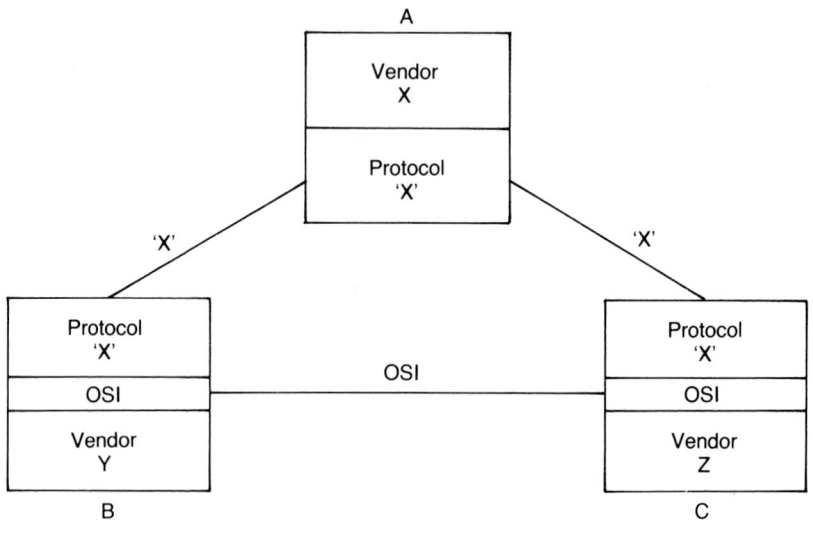

Stage 1: (1983 to 1986)

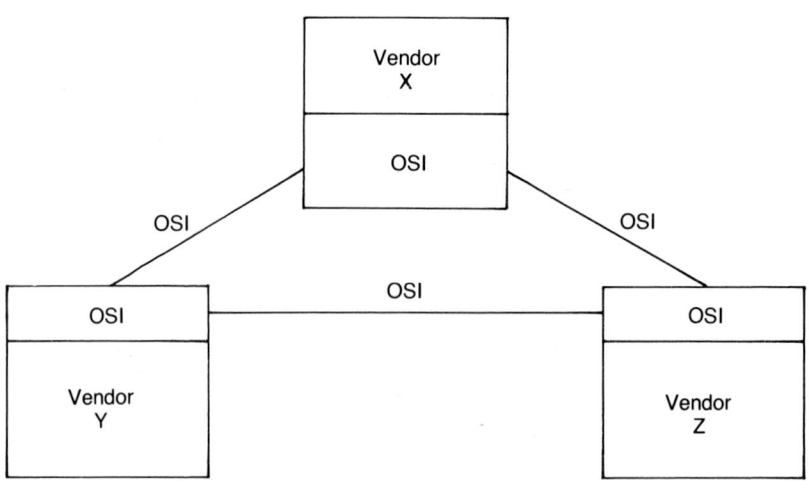

Stage 2: (1986 onwards)

Figure 9.1 Staged Approach to OSI

A STRATEGIC PLAN

commonality of needs in the infrastructure. Users can confidently include in their strategy towards open networking the route being established by ISO with its OSI recommendations. A gradual adoption of OSI interlinking and interworking protocols in place of proprietary protocols should be undertaken.

By 1986 and onwards, the aim should be to gradually replace all proprietary communications protocols with their OSI equivalents. Today proprietary equipment is likely to form the mainstay of any procurement strategy; once OSI standards are established the way is open to the interconnection of other suppliers' equipment.

As a deliberate policy, development of in-house OSI protocol packages should be discouraged. Packages should only be taken from manufacturers as they become available and only when fully supported.

Consolidate all Separate Data Networks

To reverse the direction of the existing ad-hoc approach to communications development and to remove the problems that consequentially arise, planners today need a convincing and well co-ordinated plan to entice individual data network users to adopt a common network strategy.

Such a strategy must necessitate the coming together of separate application-dependent data networks into a single, integrated, corporate network.

Such a move would enable the achievement of:

— lower transmission costs through sharing costly transmission and switching resources;

— increased flexibility in configuring network applications;

— common network interfaces encouraging the shared use of data;

— increased functionality of the network.

The first step in this direction could include a move towards packet switching through the adoption of X.25 and the setting up of an experimental private X.25 network to support suitable applications which are currently resident on several independent networks. Justification for such a move would be increased efficiency resulting from the use of shared network resources, and increased flexibility to meet growth in traffic and new applications. A packet switched data network also provides the opportunity to introduce ISO standards through the adoption of X.25 into the transport network, thereby moving towards an open network architecture.

In-house developments will concentrate on the optimisation of X.25 to encourage individual network users to fully utilise the common network strategy, and the enhancement of PAD parameters and user interfaces.

Although the development of a private X.25 network is valid today, the option to move towards the PSS network should be retained and continuously reviewed against changes in PSS tariffs and network enhancements such as those outlined in Chapter 4.

Open up the Data Network

The consolidation of data traffic onto a single network paves the way for the organisation to add text (electronic mail) traffic onto the same network. It also provides the opportunity to introduce gateways from the private network onto the public network (PSS). Two developments provide an impetus to the requirement for private data networks to interconnect with public packet switching networks (PSS): first the increase in the number and size of private data networks; and second, the maturing of national data networks (with standard X.25 interfaces and international X.75 interconnections) which offers new opportunities for national and worldwide interconnection.

The purpose and degree of interconnection will vary considerably. For example, one user may require interworking with a number of domestic and international public packet switched networks for extended geographic coverage. Another may specify interconnection with public networks for automatic back-up of private network facilities. Others may wish to interconnect via X.25 with public networks or provide connection for support of proprietary terminals.

Public network access can be identified as providing the benefits

A STRATEGIC PLAN

of increased geographic coverage, extra capacity to meet peak demands, or low-cost back-up. In some instances, the public network may provide a cost-effective means of interconnection between private network sites.

A number of commercial reasons may arise for the interconnection of private network sites. For small private networks requiring wide geographic coverage with low data volumes, long-haul transmission over PSS may be cheaper than dedicated facilities. Dedicated links on heavily used routes can be supplemented with public network switched connections to permit economical wide geographic coverage. The tariff structures might discourage the use of leased lines in favour of public data networks (PSS and ISDN).

Although explicit standards for the interconnection between private and public packet switched networks are still under study, X.25 can be used effectively to provide standard gateways to public networks. The additional capability can be implemented in the private network utilising the facilities of the stored program-control PABX (see Chapter 6).

Exploit the New Opportunities

The major objective for any strategy is that, above everything else, it must always be sufficient for business requirements. Hence the need for commitment from top management and the establishment of a mechanism for tying the strategy into the overall business plan. One danger which has emerged in the past has been the difficulties which have resulted from becoming locked into in-house technical solutions. This has been referred to with respect to proprietary data networks but in a similar manner can be identified in most areas of computing and communications; for example, in the development of large in-house centralised computing resources. One primary reason for this situation is the manifestation of in-house technical know-how and the idolisation of new technology for better or for worse.

The temptation to exploit technology for technology's sake is clearly to be avoided: business needs, not technology, must always be the driving force. An example of this might occur in communications where a company becomes locked into private networks irrespective of changing business requirements.

It is therefore important, when the stage of detailed planning is reached, to realise that the main objective is to exploit the advantages of all the opportunities which lead to an improvement in business effectiveness; not, say, solely to be a provider of private networks. This means that the detailed planning should be very closely related to the developments in the outside world.

Watch BT

Now and in the foreseeable future, British Telecom has a high-technology planning function with respect to UK telecommunications, and this will continue to have a major influence on all organisations. Hence considerable attention should be given to current BT policy when establishing the future strategy for investment in, and adoption of, new technology for both UK and worldwide communications.

Hence the proposed strategy recommends that the organisation should follow BT policy as closely as possible, provided it matches business needs. Current BT strategy and, to a lesser degree, Mercury communications strategy reside in the ultimate integration of services through ISDN (see Chapter 5) which will provide a single public switched digital network throughout the UK. The key elements in BT plans to modernise its public network are the installation of System X, the digitisation of the trunk network, and ultimately the digitisation of local ends.

Plan for Integration/ISDN

Consideration of this policy indicates that, on the longer timescale, organisations should plan for the ultimate integration of wide-area communications services onto a single digital network and the provision of voice switching through public (System X) exchanges. However, the widespread introduction of System X and ISDN facilities is unlikely within a ten-year timescale and at present they are limited by a number of obstacles of which costs and lack of international digital switching standards seem to be the most significant.

Nevertheless, the programme is gaining momentum through

A STRATEGIC PLAN

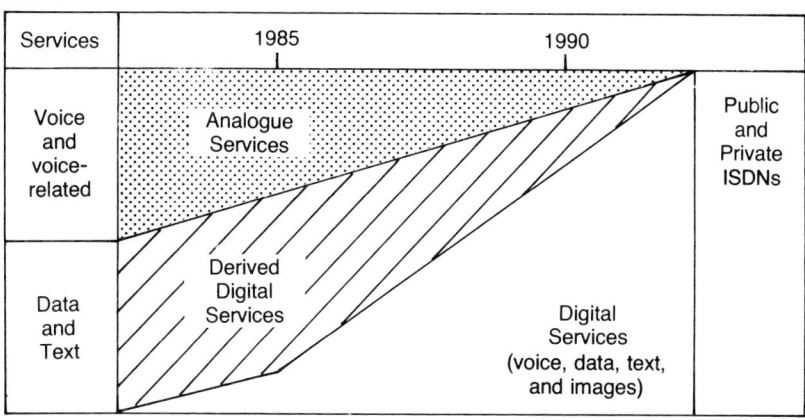

Figure 9.2 Plan for Integration

acceleration of the System X programme, the development of integrated digital networking facilities, and greater activity on the ISDN standards front. The launching of the ISDN pilot service in 1984 is particularly significant as it provides the opportunity to gain operational experience of voice, text, and data integration.

An overall plan for the integration of voice, text and data services therefore suggests a gradual migration towards the adoption of ISDN and corporate integrated networks by the early 1990s (see Figure 9.2).

In the meantime both BT and Mercury are already well advanced in the provision of dedicated high-speed digital services, and BT are continuing with the substantial expansion of the PSS network to meet demands for specialised data services.

Go Digital

Today the organisation should plan to capitalise on the network advances that BT and Mercury are offering by transferring, within a five-year framework, not less than, say, half of the corporate network to digital switching and transmission and, at the same time, make more extensive use of the new switched network facilities which can offer lower cost and greater flexibility of operation.

Migration to full digital working is likely to be limited by existing investments and commitments, for example, existing voice exchanges acquired on a ten year write-off basis. Such circumstances will create a need in the interim period for bridges to existing systems; for example, message switch, viewdata, computer.

Digital communications is cheaper than analogue because it offers much increased traffic capacity and uses micro chip technology and simplified interfaces. Most significant cost reductions can be shown for data transmission because digital operation is the natural mode of working, removing the necessity for the complexity of modems, etc. For example, KiloStream can reduce the cost of high-speed data circuits by up to 75%.

However, it is important to appreciate that the full potential of such cost savings can only be realised once the fully digital system is operational. For the existing public networks this is a lengthy process, as illustrated in Chapter 4 where BT and Mercury plans for availability of digital services were outlined. For private networks a concentrated programme of digitisation is likely to take three to five years to complete.

Sensible use of existing assets and an orderly transition to the new methods of working are fundamental requirements. For example, a typical programme for the replacement of analogue exchanges by an increasing number of digital exchanges, together with the replacement of analogue widebands by MegaStream high-capacity digital circuits, might be undertaken as shown in the various parts of Figure 9.3.

SUB-STRATEGIES

Voice Services

The strategy for voice systems is clear: gradually migrate from analogue to digital switching and transmission by taking the opportunity to replace existing voice switches by new SPC digital exchanges, and take advantage of the BT and Mercury offerings to provide a more cost-effective digital network. In many organisa-

A STRATEGIC PLAN

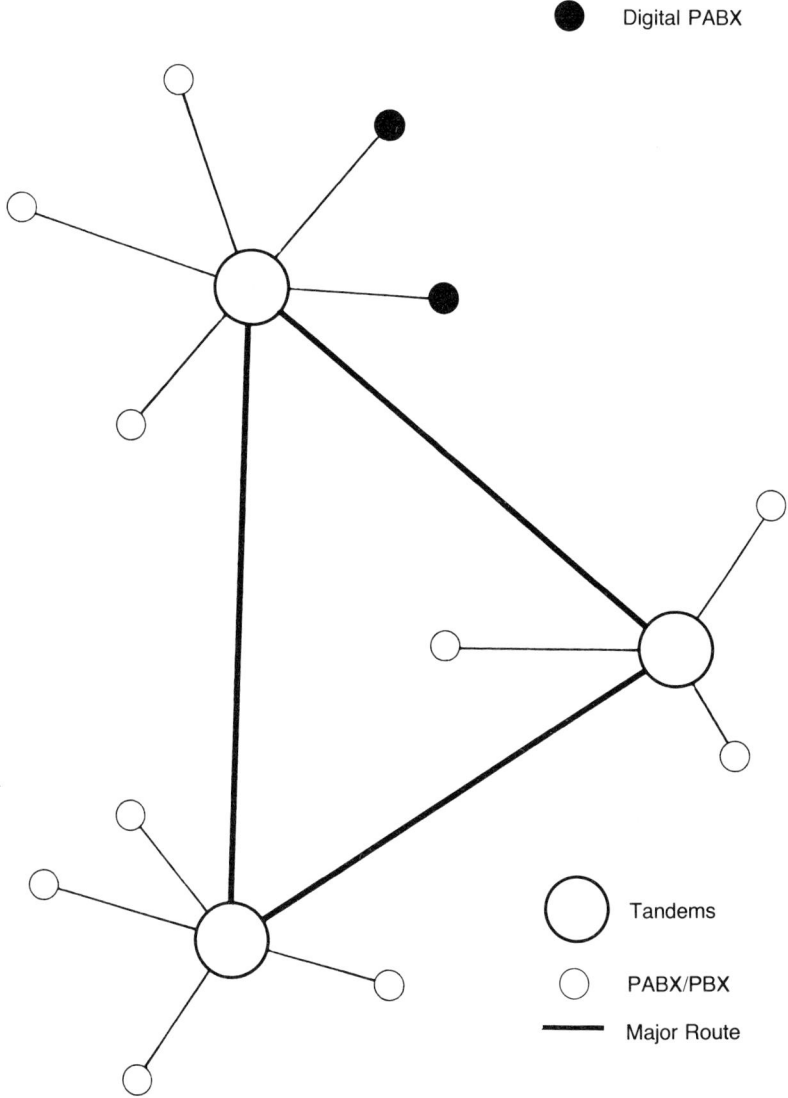

Figure 9.3a Speech Network Major Routes (1983)

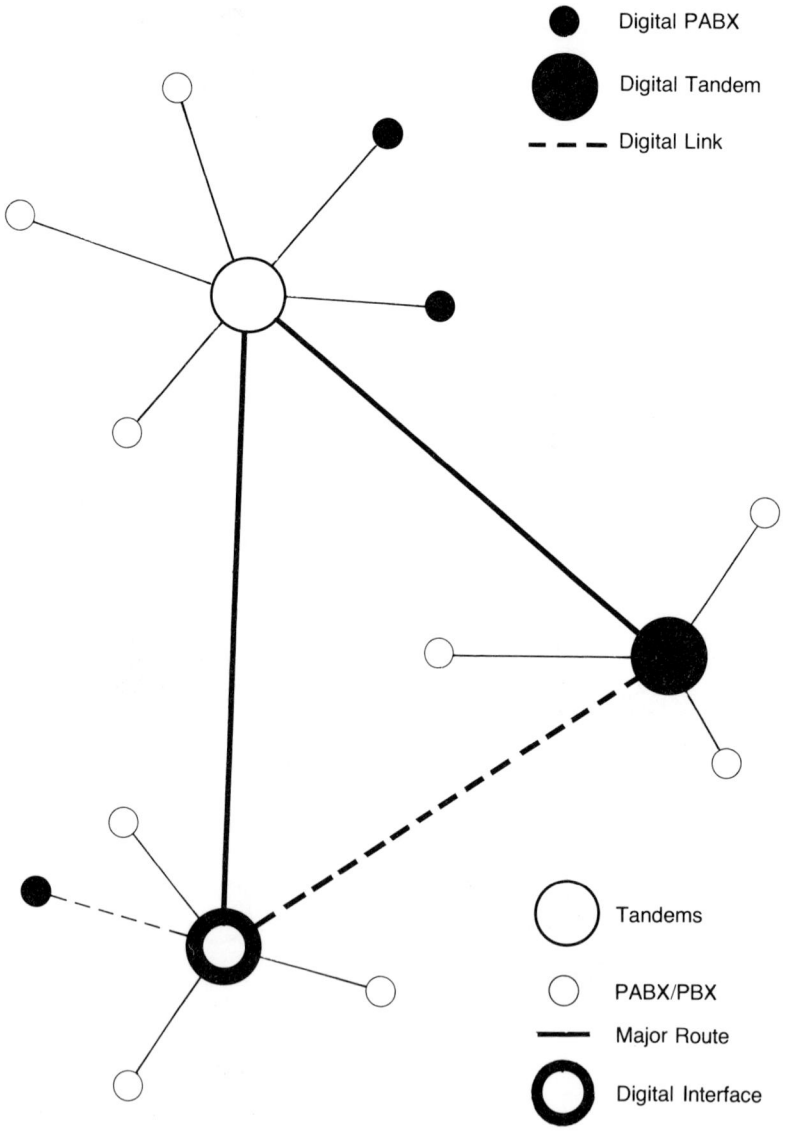

Figure 9.3b   Stage 1: (1983/84)

A STRATEGIC PLAN

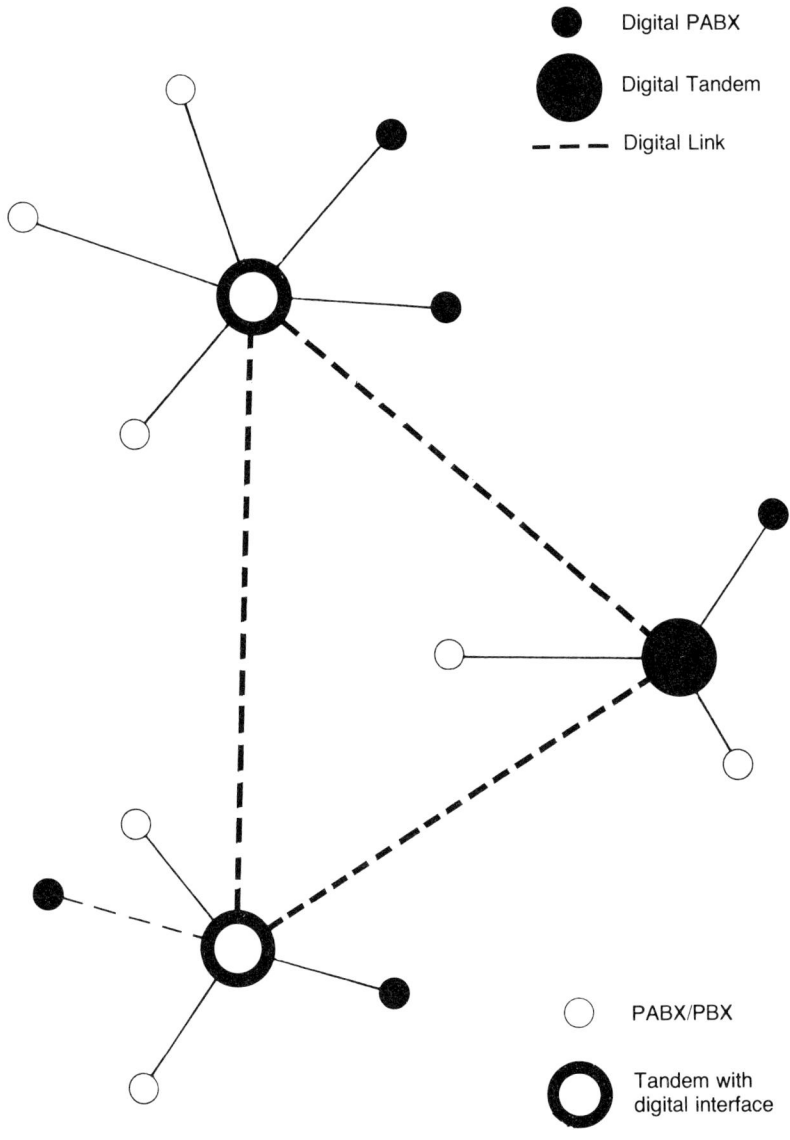

Figure 9.3c   Stage 2: (1984/85)

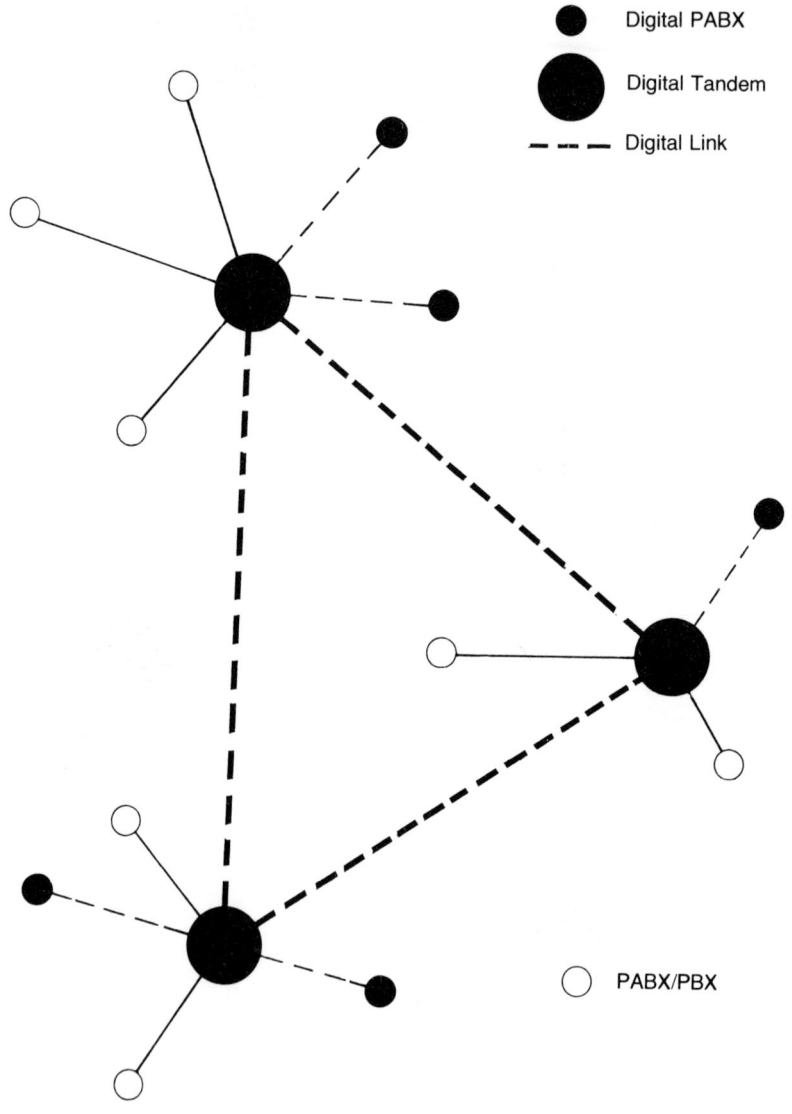

Figure 9.3d Stage 3: (1985/86)

A STRATEGIC PLAN

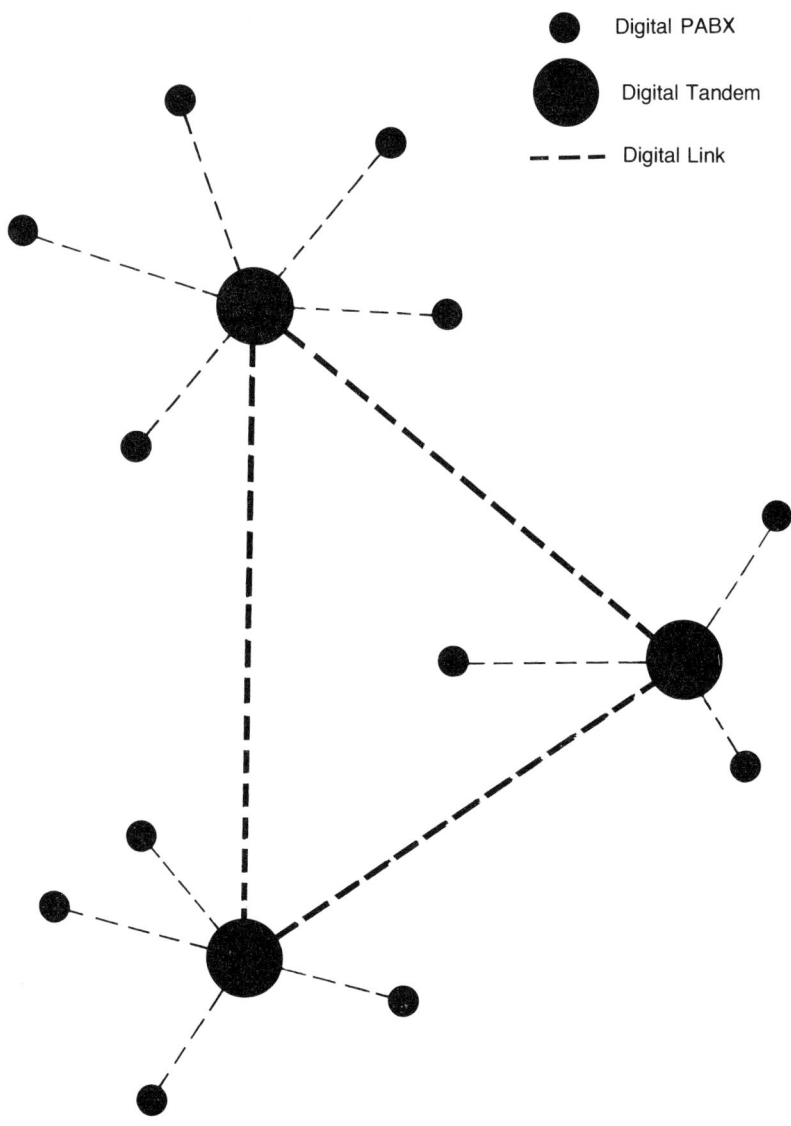

Figure 9.3e   Stage 4: (1986/87)

tions the requirement will be to replace FDM wideband long-haul links by 30-channel PCM digital leased lines provided that the replacement is cost justified and is not prevented by the restrictions of provisioning clauses on existing widebands.

The provision of high-speed digital links which effectively give greater bandwidth at less cost provides an opportunity for further developments which utilise the spare capacity. This will obviously include the 'piggy-backing' of other data and text services onto the wideband links where the topologies of the individual networks coincide; although this may become less attractive if the cost of digital connections continues to fall, thereby lessening the economies of scale advantage. This can be seen today in the provision of KiloStream links which are available at less than half the cost of traditional low-speed analogue circuits over all but the shortest distances, and considerably more for higher speeds.

More importantly the availability of cheaper bandwidth opens up the way for wide area integration of voice, data and text services and opportunities for new services apart from voice, such as video conferencing. This opportunity is considerably enhanced by the compression of voice into a bandwidth of 32 Kbit/s today and the likelihood of 16 Kbit/s tomorrow and the availability of digital channel multiplexers (as discussed in Chapter 4).

To exploit these advantages, the strategy should therefore make provision for a small proportion of the annual communications budget to be invested in pilot schemes in areas such as videotex, voice storage and message services, or 2 Mbit/s video conferencing as appropriate to the objectives of the overall IT strategy. Such an approach will encourage the promotion of a wider acceptance of such services within the organisation and, at the same time, provide the opportunity to gain sight of the issues and problems associated with the introduction of the new concepts and techniques. However, a primary aim would be to be in a position to facilitate the rapid take-up of these technologies as the price, performance and reliability indices become favourable to the organisation's particular situation.

Data Services

Data communications strategy will revolve around a move towards the adoption of layered protocols such as X.25, provision of private packet switched networks and development of private/public network gateways. This approach will encourage the coming together of application-dependent data networks and will signpost the direction towards an open network architecture of the future. This is an essential component of the overall IT strategy. At the same time, the opportunity will be taken to move away from analogue services and to eventually replace all connections by high-speed, digital links using both leased line services (BT MegaStream and KiloStream, and Mercury) and/or digital switched services (BT ISDN) and satellite services.

The incorporation of satellite communication into the private network adds a new dimension to the services and facilities provided by the network which, together with high-speed digital terrestrial links, provides the higher bandwidths required for specialised applications such as computer-aided design, newsprint transmission and video conferencing.

A Degree of Integration

Voice systems will increasingly be required to support text and data applications although, as was discussed earlier, the widespread integration of such services in which voice, data, text and perhaps video and facsimile traffic is transmitted simultaneously is unlikely much before the end of the decade. Today the opportunity to provide a degree of voice and data integration through the new generation of PABXs is there, although at a cost. In the immediate future, full end-to-end digital working will emerge on PABXs which, together with the eventual availability of multi-function workstations, the development of digital signalling standards and the growth of the digital network, will create a total digital environment.

Until that time, the opportunities for supporting text and data applications on voice networks should be exploited for the reasons given earlier; for example, to provide more cost-effective communications with enhanced facilities; to provide the flexibility to meet increased demands through changing situations; and to benefit from the economies of scale of large networks. However, the primary aim should be to be in a position to facilitate the rapid take-up of full integration when it eventually becomes a viable solution.

The capacity of the network in terms of volumes of traffic is dependent upon the switching capacity of the PABX. This is currently constrained by the technology in use although this obstacle will eventually disappear with the introduction of non-blocking systems. Because it is essential to identify any capacity problems through data occupancy of the PABX, initially the data handling capability is likely to be restricted to low-speed low-volume applications, typified by the connection of local enquiry-processing data terminals. Such an arrangement, which will facilitate low-volume digital switching of data (with its corresponding savings on modems), also provides for the digital connection of other devices (such as communicating word processors) into the message switched network. This provides for internal electronic mail/text services with future opportunities for the development of connections into the public telex network through gateways in the PABX, and the possibility of the connection of facsimile equipment at a later date.

Such applications should be introduced on the basis of pilot schemes initially set up on an experimental basis. These will provide the opportunity to gain operational experience of voice, text and data integration. Development of the network will occur as necessary in accordance with the organisation's overall IT strategy but in any case with a deliberate slow loading of the PABX to minimise occupancy problems. This may change in the light of user operational experience and the philosophy adopted by manufacturers in their approach towards the 'electronic office'.

Apart from the occupancy problem, other reasons for maintaining a segregated, high-speed, large-volume data transfer facility include:

— bulk volume data transfers are usually only required over fixed routes; therefore there is no need for switching;

— switching of high-speed data necessitates error correction techniques to avoid the loss of data; such techniques are not yet available on digital PABXs;

— current digital PABX design with automatic changeover to

a standby processor creates significant data loss problems when handling data at high speeds; improved switching techniques are required;

— present-day data rates on PABXs (ie 9.6/19.2 Kbit/s for analogue extensions; 64 Kbit/s for digital extensions) may be inadequate.

Today the requirements for large-volume, high-speed data communications will continue to be met by dedicated wideband and/or high-speed digital circuits between nodes using existing connections. However, the use of more and more high-speed digital services and digital multiplexers will provide high-capacity, cost-efficient backbone routes for multiple service digital data and voice networks of the future.

THE STRATEGY IN BRIEF

The content of the strategy outlined in the previous sections is summarised as follows:

Overall Strategy

— migrate to OSI;

— consolidate existing separate data networks into single network;

— open up the data network;

— exploit the new opportunities, by:

— watching BT;

— planning for integration/ISDN;

— migrating from analogue to digital.

Sub-Strategies

Voice

— go digital;

— exploit the bandwidth;

— introduce a degree of integration.

Data

— move towards X.25;

— go digital;

— explore the opportunities for high-speed digital transmission.

WHICH FIRST?

In preparing a strategy for the wide area network, first priority must be given to voice traffic as being the dominant communications medium in all organisations, and likely to remain so in the foreseeable future. This implies that the most significant part of the future technical strategy is the upgrading of the network to digital working in parallel with the developments in the public network. As discussed earlier, this involves implementation by choosing digital PABXs wherever possible, by providing PCM digital links throughout the country to replace the FDM groups, and introducing digital main tandem centres when replacement is possible. Current PABX-supplier and BT plans suggest that some UK private voice networks could become digital by the mid-eighties.

This will establish a transport network for digital local switches to be interlinked and provide an infrastructure for all forms of communications (voice and non-voice) from 1985 onwards (Figure 9.4). For example, end-to-end connection of low-volume data traffic becomes possible as digital PABXs are introduced at local sites.

Having converted the voice network from analogue to digital, it is now possible to overlay the data network onto the voice network. This can be done by, for example, interlinking packet switching nodes at local sites through digital circuits derived from the wide area voice network. Such a strategy acknowledges the advantages of an intelligent network in terms of in-built resilience, error-free transmission and flexible user access, and takes advantage of shared transport facilities.

In practice, however, although a packet switched network is appropriate for many data processing applications, it tends not to be a viable solution for remote job entry in which the use of

A STRATEGIC PLAN

Figure 9.4   An Integrated Communications Network for the Future

high-cost equipment for large volumes of infrequent traffic is not attractive. In these circumstances a dedicated or point-to-point service will still have a place in the overall network design. Hence the data network is likely to comprise both dedicated and packet switched connections as well as the end-to-end circuit switched data connections referred to earlier.

PRIVATE OR PUBLIC ISDN NETWORKS?

The concept of an integrated services PABX – in the sense of a digital PABX with connections into the public ISDN through IDA – promises to extend some of the benefits currently enjoyed by large organisations to the medium and smaller business users. In particular, it offers the benefits of a greatly improved telephone service through the use of more efficient and faster transmission and signalling, and economy in the uses of lines by sharing them amongst a number of services.

At the same time, it also raises an interesting alternative option for planners of large corporate networks faced with the problems of operating and developing a private integrated services network. ISDN will tend to remove one of the major reasons for the historical development of private networks in the UK; ie the shortcomings of the public network.

As BT continues to introduce public data services in the UK (as also may Mercury), organisations will need to make a choice between public and private network facilities. However, two very significant factors may favour private networks. Firstly, it is unlikely that large organisations will wish to lose control of their own communications resources; and it is also unlikely that public data services will be able to offer more than basic transport and network facilities, given the vastly differing needs of individual users at the application level.

But perhaps more significantly, the current UK regulatory environment is generating more competition which will lead to dramatic changes within the private network market. Very noticeable, even at the early stages of liberalisation, is the dramatic release of cheap digital bandwidth, by both BT and Mercury, to users of private networks and the upsurge in the number of PABX suppliers and systems coming onto the market.

In the competitive network environment of the UK, the marketplace now dominates. It remains to be seen whether an ISDN can compete economically with separate and specialised networks orientated towards specific user needs.

Bibliography

Anderson G M, Day J F and Spindel L A, A Communications Protocol for Integrated Voice and Data Service in the Business Office, *Proc. 6th Int. Conf. Computer Communication (ICCC)*, Sept 1982.

Baker T W, The Evolution of Private Communications, *Electronics and Power*, June 1982.

Bingham J E and Davies G W P, *Planning for Data Communications*, The MacMillan Press Ltd, 1977.

Bleazard G B, *Why Packet Switching?*, NCC Publications, 1982.

Bleazard G B, *Evaluating Data Transmission Services*, NCC Publications, 1983.

Cott P J, Business Demand for Digital Telecoms: an Integrated System Approach, *Proc. Int. Business Telecom. Conf.*, 1983.

Cronshaw D, Microwave Communications, *Communicate*, July/Aug 1982.

Dewis I G, An Information Communications Strategy, *Proc. 6th Int. Conf. Computer Communication (ICCC)*, Sept 1982.

Edwards P, Data Network Planning, *Systems International*, Jan 1983.

Firth R J, *Managing Viewdata Systems*, NCC Publications, 1983.

Gee K C E, *Local Area Networks*, NCC Publications, 1982.

Handbook of Data Communications, NCC Publications, 1982.

Hardy J H M and Hoppitt C E, Access to British Telecom ISDN, *Proc. 6th Int. Conf. Computer Communication (ICCC)*, Sept 1982.

Hardy P, *Digital Private Circuits for Telecommunications*, NCC Publications, 1984.

Hart M, A Migratory Path Towards Voice and Data Integration, *Proc. Int. Business Telecom. Conf.*, 1983.

Integrated Voice/Data Communications: Slowly Evolving, *Telecommunications*, May 1983.

Introducing Computerised Telephone Switchboards (PABXs), NCC Publications, 1982.

Jeanes D L, Interconnection of Public and Private Networks, *Proc. 6th Int. Conf. Computer Communication (ICCC)*, Sept 1982.

Lane J E, *A Review of British Telecom Services*, NCC Publications, 1982.

Leighfield J P, Some Guidelines for Harnessing the New Opportunities, *Proc. Int. Business Telecom. Conf.*, 1983.

Merging Voice and Data, *Telecommunications*, Oct 1982.

O'Hara S, Business Implications of New Telecoms Services, *Proc. Int. Business Telecom. Conf.*, 1983.

Price S G, *Introducing the Electronic Office*, NCC Publications, 1982.

Price S G, *Preparing for Teletex*, NCC Publications, 1982.

Pritchard J A T and Wilson P A, *Planning Office Automation – Electronic Message Systems*, NCC Publications, 1982.

Pritchard J A T and Cole I, *Planning Office Automation – Information Management Systems*, NCC Publications, 1983.

Project Universe, *Communications Management*, May 1983.

Rybczynski A M and Chow A C, Voice/Data Integration Opportunities, *Proc. 6th Int. Conf. Computer Communication (ICCC)*, Sept 1982.

Scott P R D, *Reviewing Your Data Transmission Network*, NCC Publications, 1983.

Williams B O B, Organising for Information Technology, *Proc. Int. Business Telecom. Conf.*, 1983.

Index

backward channels	18
bridges	114
British Telecom (BT)	28, 31-33, 35, 40, 45, 48, 112, 114
burst mode techniques	57
bus networks	72
business communications	81
call-based services	56
call information logging	16, 21
carrier services	31
CCITT	27, 40, 45, 46, 53, 54, 58, 62, 75, 76, 100
centralisation and control	88
circuit switching	53, 54, 57, 58
Closed User Groups	27
common channel signalling	58, 64, 100
communicating word processing	24, 26
conferencing	24, 47
Confravision	28, 48
Corporate Telecommunications Planning Group	86
cost-effectiveness	18
cost question	22
costs	21
data communications	13, 30, 56, 70
data compression	38

data networks   16, 22, 25, 33, 54, 55, 70,
                                        76, 109, 110
data processing   18, 25
data transmission   18, 19, 41
Datel   42
dial-up
 — data communications   18
 — over PSTN   26
digital
 — data channel   37
 — encoding   42, 49, 51, 99
 — exchanges   31, 114
 — fax   26
 — PABX   97-100, 124
 — private network   35, 37, 40, 42
 — services   21, 101
 — signalling standards   121
 — switching   35, 45, 70, 98, 113
 — transmission   31, 35, 113
Digital Access Signalling
  System (DASS)   64, 66, 99
Digital Private Network Signalling
  System (DPNSS)   100
digitisation   31, 51, 56, 103
distributed
 — minis   16
 — processors   13, 55
distributed processing (PABX)   72, 99

E&M trunks   74
echo cancelling   57
economies of scale   18, 120, 121
electronic
 — exchanges   16
 — mail   13, 26
 — message systems   26, 33
encoding   70

facsimile   16, 24, 26, 27, 30, 70
FDM links   39

gateways	28, 33, 101, 110, 121, 122
high-speed data links	37, 123
image communications	70
impact on communications services	29
in-band signalling	42, 58
information	13
information technology (IT)	81
Integrated Digital Access (IDA)	35, 61-66, 76, 100, 126
Integrated Digital Network (IDN)	59, 99
integrated networks	42, 75-76, 95
integrated office	23
Integrated Services Digital Network (ISDN)	32, 35, 45, 51-54, 57, 58, 61, 62, 64, 75, 76, 97, 99, 112, 126
integrated services, evolution of	96-99
Integrated Services PBX (ISPBX)	66
integration	95, 112, 121-123
— data services	95
— image	96
— in private networks	76-79
— of all services	32, 70-74, 90, 106
— text	96, 120
— voice and data	20, 54-56, 58, 69, 75, 76, 96, 98, 101, 120, 121
intercept strategy	94
interconnection	110, 111
interfaces	58, 62
interfacing	27, 53, 58
International Packet Switched Service (IPSS)	33
InterStream One	33
ISO	76, 94, 95, 101, 106-109
KiloStream	35, 40, 42, 59, 114
leased circuits	33, 35
liberalisation	126

local area networks	13, 100, 101
London Overlay	37, 39
mainframes	13, 16
management control facilities	22
MegaStream	35, 37, 39, 42, 49, 59, 114
MegaStream 2 multiplexer	38
Mercury Communications	32, 43, 58, 114
message switching	13, 16, 18, 46, 48, 58
micro (computers)	25
mixed-mode operation	27
MODEC	64
modem pools	74
multi-line	66
multiplexer	37, 42, 51, 103
multiplexing	57
multipoint	16
National Digital Private Circuit Network (NDPCN)	59
network	
— control	18
— management	18, 56
— management and control	77
— planning	16
— services	18, 59
— switching data and voice	77
Network Terminating Equipment (NTE)	62, 64
Network Terminating Unit (NTU)	40
new opportunities	111-114
non-blocking systems	122
occupancy	122
office automation	25, 70
office communications	69
open integrated network	91, 93, 101-103
Open Systems Interconnection (OSI)	93, 94, 96, 101, 106-109
Operational Management Group	88-90

INDEX

optical fibres	35, 43
Orator	49
organisational	
— changes	18
— issues	83
— problems	103
— structure and staffing	86-90
organising for IT	84-85
PABX	13, 23, 32, 37, 39, 46, 48, 58, 67, 72, 74, 76, 100, 101, 111, 121, 122
PABX facilities	77
packet switching	
— network	32, 74, 109, 110, 124
— services	54, 57, 58
Packet SwitchStream (PSS)	33, 46
PCM	43, 51, 53, 57, 70, 74, 99, 120, 124
personal computing	16, 29
pilot schemes	120, 122
planning	25, 26
point-to-point circuits	16, 39
Prestel	27
private	
— carrier services	22
— circuit	17, 19, 40
— ISDN networks	100, 126-127
— packet switched networks	120-121
process control	28, 30
Project Universe	101
protocol conversion	46, 47, 75, 101
protocols	58, 76
PSS	33, 35, 110, 111
PSTN	18, 33, 46
PTTs	32, 55
public carrier services	21, 22
rate adaptor	62
ring networks	72

satellites	19, 67
SatStream	35, 43
signalling	31, 53, 57, 58
spare capacity	23
standards	93
standards (fax)	26
star networks	72
statistical multiplexers	18
store-and-forward	27, 77
stored program control (SPC)	
— exchanges	46, 74, 114
— PABX	24
— switchboards	21
strategic	
— issues	85
— plan	105-127
strategy	20, 24, 81-103
— data services	120-121, 124-126
— voice services	114-120, 124
structured channels	39, 40
System X	32, 35, 61, 64, 76, 99
tandem switches	16, 77, 124
tariff	39, 42
teleconferencing	21, 48, 49
telephone bill	23
telephone network	31, 57
Teletex	13, 26, 27, 30, 32, 33, 45, 46
telex	13, 16, 26, 27, 30, 33, 45, 46
telex message switching	24
terminals	13, 16, 25-27, 53, 55, 62
text communications	26, 30
text networks	22
timescales	23
traffic	
— loads	21
— monitoring	16
— volumes	16

INDEX 137

transmission	57
trends	55, 57, 58
trunks	32, 57
unstructured channels	39, 40
video	70
video conferencing	28, 30, 48, 49
VideoStream	28, 49
videotex	27, 28
viewdata	13, 18, 27, 30
virtual channels	77
voice	
— channel	38, 43
— communications	13, 25, 29, 40, 56, 114
— networks	16, 22, 54, 76
— store-and-forward	16
wideband	
— circuits	18, 39, 43, 123
— links	16, 18, 114
— services	21
word processors	26, 46
workstation	46, 48, 70, 75, 121
X Stream	32, 35, 39, 40, 43
X.3/28/29	33
X.21	39, 40, 54, 103
X.21 bis	39, 40
X.25	33, 54, 58, 67, 74, 109, 110, 120